解读《跟单信用证统一惯例（2007年修订本）》第600号出版物

主　编　陈国武
副主编　王伟铭　王　虹
参　编　李　文　郑　颖
　　　　　樊　薇　田　莽
　　　　　陈连莹

天津大学出版社
TIANJIN UNIVERSITY PRESS

图书在版编目(CIP)数据

解读《跟单信用证统一惯例(2007年修订本)》第600号出版物/陈国武主编.—天津:天津大学出版社,2007.4

ISBN 978-7-5618-2431-3

Ⅰ.解… Ⅱ.陈… Ⅲ.国际结算—信用证—学习参考资料 Ⅳ.F830.73

中国版本图书馆CIP数据核字(2007)第037404号

出版发行	天津大学出版社
出 版 人	杨 欢
地 址	天津市卫津路92号天津大学内(邮编:300072)
电 话	发行部:022-27403647 邮购部:022-27402742
印 刷	昌黎太阳红彩色印刷有限责任公司
经 销	全国各地新华书店
开 本	148mm×210mm
印 张	6.25
字 数	194千
版 次	2007年4月第1版
印 次	2007年4月第1次
印 数	1-8 000
定 价	23.00元

前　言

自上世纪初跟单信用证问世以来，信用证一直是国际贸易中使用最为广泛的支付方式之一。在我国，用于进出口贸易的多种支付方式中，跟单信用证方式占很大比重。但是，由于这种支付方式相对比较复杂，在使用过程中，经常会出现这样或那样的问题，有的会造成不良影响，甚至造成经济上的损失。究其原因，主要还是对于这种支付方式的含义及作用缺乏深入了解所致。因此，学习、研究和了解这种支付方式的基本原理，有关各方当事人的权利和义务，以及若干条款、名词和术语解释，进而掌握这个在国际上已经形成的、并为银行界及贸易界普遍承认和使用的跟单信用证统一惯例，无疑是十分必要的。

《跟单信用证统一惯例（1993 年修订本）》第 500 号出版物使用十余年后，从 2007 年 7 月起，被《跟单信用证统一惯例（2007 年修订本）》第 600 号出版物所代替。在第 600 号出版物从讨论稿到正式文件公布的过程中，我们一直采用“三结合”（指由具有对外贸易实践经验和多年教授国际结算等课程的高校教师、银行具有国际结算实践经验的人员，以及英语较好、以对外贸易实务为研究方向的在校高年级研究生组成）的办法来学习、研究和理解它。目的是通过集体学习和研究，掌握信用证国际惯例的内涵，能比较灵活地运用它，力争拉近高校专业教育和社会实践之间的距离，为我国尽快从贸易大国提升为贸易强国贡献绵薄之力。

陈国武教授在比较中、英文版本的新、旧出版物基础上，解读第 600 号出版物，并对历次出版物的内容进行了简要介绍。全书由陈国武教授总纂。

由于编者的水平有限，本书难免存在缺点和错误，敬请读者不吝批评和指正。

编者

2007年2月

目　录

第一部分　讲解 UCP600

第二部分 简介《跟单信用证统一惯例》历次出版物主要内容

第一部分　讲解 UCP600

[原文] Article 1　Application of UCP

The Uniform Customs and Practice for Documentary Credits, 2007 Revision, ICC Publication no. 600 ("UCP") are rules that apply to any documentary credit ("credit") (including, to the extent to which they may be applicable, any standby letter of credit) when the text of the credit expressly indicates that it is subject to these rules. They are binding on all parties thereto unless expressly modified or excluded by the credit.

[译文] 第一条　统一惯例的适用范围

跟单信用证统一惯例，2007 年修订本，国际商会第 600 号出版物（简称 "UCP"），适用于任何正文中标明受本惯例约束的跟单信用证简称 "信用证"（包括在本惯例适用范围内的备用信用证）。除非在信用证中被明确地修改或排除，本惯例对一切有关当事人均具有约束力。

[讲解]

1.2007 年修订的跟单信用证统一惯例第 600 号出版物对任何跟单信用证都适用。

2. 本惯例不仅对随附货运单据的跟单信用证适用，也对在本惯例范围内的、不随附货运单据的备用信用证适用。

3. 为什么惯例特别提出备用信用证呢？因为本惯例是 "跟

单信用证统一惯例”，指在一般情况下，证内的受益人要获得相应的款项时，必须向银行提供符合信用证内所规定的、包括货运单据在内的全套单据。而备用信用证却并非如此，根据它的特点，它是依附于某种支付方式（例如托收方式）而使用、作为履行某种职责的保障。例如，买卖双方在一笔交易中采用托收方式，卖方担心货物装运后不能收回货款，要求买方在货物装运前向其开出备用信用证作为保障。后来，卖方将货物装出后，买方由于各种原因，拒绝到进口地银行付款赎单。在这种情况下，如果没有备用信用证，卖方必然会遭受一定损失（如将货物另行转售、原船运回、降价销售甚至全部货款落空），但在卖方收到备用信用证才发货的要求下，问题的处理就大不相同。这时的卖方，可以根据证内规定索款的办法，向开证行索取货款，因而不受损失。由此可见，备用信用证的付款要求，虽不像跟单信用证那样，要求“单单相符”、“单证相符”，但由于两种信用证都是“银行信用”，银行处于“第一性”的地位。这就需要有一个适当的惯例来约束它们。这就是为什么“跟单信用证”的惯例强调也适用于“不跟单”的备用信用证的主要原因。

4. 本惯例强调适用于备用信用证的另一方面是：虽然银行对备用信用证不涉及单据，特别是货运单据。但是，由于这种信用证的性质是银行信用。所以，凡是惯例对跟单信用证内有关当事人的约束，如在备用信用证内没有特别规定，同样也对证内的有关当事人（如开证人、开证行、通知行、受益人等），具有约束力。

[与第500号出版物比较]

本条涉及第500号出版物的第一条。

1. 本条规定：本惯例适合“任何”（any）跟单信用证，代替第500号出版物规定：适合“所有”（all）跟单信用证。笔者认为：“any”偏重于跟单信用证个体，而“all”却是偏重于受本惯例约束的信用证整体。前者更突出信用证自身。

2. 本条用“正文中标明受本惯例约束的跟单信用证”词句，代替“在正文中表明按本惯例办理的跟单信用证”。这两句话的含义、语气和体现的作用大不相同。前者含义明确，指出受本惯例“约束”，即不得违反惯例的规定相关指示，很肯定。后者指出按本惯例“办理”，从语气、要求与前者相比，相对比较松、软一些。

3. 本条用“除非在信用证中被明确地修改或排除，本惯例对一切有关当事人均具有约束力”代替第 500 号出版物的“除非信用证中另有规定，本惯例对一切有关当事人均具有约束力”。前者语气更肯定、坚决。

[原文] Article 2　Definitions

For the purpose of these rules:

Advising bank means the bank that advises the credit at the request of the issuing bank.

Applicant means the party on whose request the credit is issued.

Banking day means a day on which a bank is regularly open at the place at which an act subject to these rules is to be performed.

Beneficiary means the party in whose favour a credit is issued.

Complying presentation means a presentation that is in accordance with the terms and conditions of the credit, the applicable provisions of these rules and international standard banking practice.

Confirmation means a definite undertaking of the confirming bank, in addition to that of the issuing bank, to honour or negotiate a complying presentation.

Confirming bank means the bank that adds its confirmation to a credit upon the issuing bank's authorization or request.

Credit means any arrangement, however named or described, that is irrevocable and thereby constitutes a definite undertaking of the issuing bank to honour a complying presentation.

Honour means:

a. to pay at sight if the credit is available by sight payment.

b. to incur a deferred payment undertaking and pay at maturity if the credit is available by deferred payment.

c. to accept a bill of exchange ("draft") drawn by the beneficiary and pay at maturity if the credit is available by acceptance.

Issuing bank means the bank that issues a credit at the request of an applicant or on its own behalf.

Negotiation means the purchase by the nominated bank of drafts (drawn on a bank other than the nominated bank) and/or documents under a complying presentation, by advancing or agreeing to advance funds to the beneficiary on or before the banking day on which reimbursement is due to the nominated bank.

Nominated bank means the bank with which the credit is available or any bank in the case of a credit available with any bank.

Presentation means either the delivery of documents under a credit to the issuing bank or nominated bank or the documents so delivered.

Presenter means a beneficiary, bank or other party that makes a presentation.

[译文] 第二条　定义

就本惯例而言：

通知行意指鉴于开证行要求通知信用证的银行。

申请人意指申请开立信用证的一方。

银行日意指银行在其营业地正常营业，按照本惯例行事的行为得以在银行履行的日子。

受益人意指开立信用证中受益的一方。

相符提示意指与信用证条款，本惯例中所适用的规定及国际标准银行实务相一致的提示。

保兑意指除开证行对相符提示做出付款或议付的承诺以外，保兑行对此做出的明确承诺。

保兑行意指在开证行的授权或请求下对信用证加具保兑的银行。

信用证意指无论其如何命名或描述的一项约定，该约定不可撤销并由此相当于开证行对于相符提示予以付款的明确承诺。

承付意指：

a. 对于即期付款信用证即期付款。

b. 对于延期付款信用证做出延期付款承诺并于到期日付款。

c. 对于承兑信用证承兑由受益人出具的汇票并于到期日付款。

开证行意指应申请人要求或代表申请人开立信用证的银行。

议付意指指定银行在其应获偿付的银行工作日当天或之前，通过对受益人预付款或者表示同意向受益人提前付款的方式购买相符提示项下的汇票（汇票付款人为被指定银行以外的银行）和/或单据。

指定银行意指信用证适用的银行，在信用证适用任何银行的情况下，任何银行均为指定银行。

交单意指信用证项下单据被提交至开证行或被指定银行，抑或按此方式提交的单据。

交单人意指发出提示的受益人、银行或第三方。

［讲解］

1. 文内“就本惯例而言”指的是：本条内对以下有关信用证内的当事人、使用的专业名词所下的定义，仅限于在本惯例的范围内，出了这个范围，就不一定是这个定义。例如本惯例第一条所指的“跟单信用证”，它是泛指任何（any）银行信用证而言，即既有随附货运单据、用于买卖货物的信用证，也包括不随附货运单据的备用信用证。但在其他场合下，信用证不是这样区分的，可以根据信用证不同的使用目的而列有多种名称的信用证。如按付款时间区分，分为即期/远期信用证。按信用证是否加具保兑，分为保兑/不保兑信用证等。而在远期付款信用证中，按是否需要受益人出具汇票，分为承兑信用证和延期（迟期）付款信用证。承兑信用证需要受益人开出以银行为付款人的汇票，经银行承兑后，持票人既可以将汇票拿到贴现市场办理贴现手续，也可以等承兑的汇票到期时，向承兑银行收款。而延期（迟期）付款信用证的受益人不用开出汇票，只须凭付款银行出具的“付款承诺”，在到期时向银行收款。

2. 本条对申请人、开证行、通知行和受益人等4个信用内最主要当事人，以及有关当事人如保兑行、被指定银行和受益人等，都作了详细解释。如对于开证行，第500号和第600号出版物都对它作了详细解释，都是指出“开证行是应申请人的要求（或申请）或代表其自身开立信用证的银行”。比起一般书籍/杂志对“开证行”的解释，多了“……或代表其自身开立信用证”这部分内容。增加解释的内容，说明开证行不仅可应开证人的请求而开立信用证，还可以为自身融资的需要而开立备用信用证。

在本条内，对信用证、提示、相符提示、保兑、议付、银行日等专有词汇，也作了相应的解释。如对于提示给银行收款的单据，本条严格规定要与信用证内规定的条件、本惯例的相关规定，以及审单标准即国际标准银行实务等三方面完全一致，否则，受益人就得不到相应的款项。

本条对保兑和保兑行的含义，作了较详细解释。当前业界对在什么情况下要加“保兑”说法不一，从而造成做法也不一致。有的进出口企业，在其出口合同中就规定对方开来的信用证，必须加具保兑。这样的规定似乎欠妥，因为双方签订交易合同时，信用证根本还未开出，更谈不上开证行是哪家。资信好、实力强的银行开来信用证，即使金额较大，也没有必要加具“保兑”，况且，通知行收到来证后，是否同意转交给受益人，也会考虑包括开证行的偿付能力在内的各种因素。因此，有无必要加具“保兑”，一般应该等到信用证开到后再作决定为宜。

3. 特别要指出的是，本条对“honour”作了详细解释。一些书刊把“honour”译为“兑付”，也有的译为“付款”。在香港地区，部分银行在开立中文或中英文对照的信用证中，大多把“honour”译为“付款”。“honour”究竟应译成什么为好？笔者认为，译为“付款”更加贴切，因为本条对“honour”一词的含义，作了三点解释，即：

（1）对即期信用证即期付款；

（2）对延期（迟期）付款信用证发出付款承诺并于到期时付款；

（3）对承兑信用证承兑受益人出具的汇票并于到期时付款。

由此可见，如将“honour”翻译为“兑付”，似乎容易理解为将“承兑”和“付款”合为一个词。而实际上，在上述三大类信用证（即期、延期（迟期）和承兑信用证）中，需要办理承兑手续的，只有一种。此外，无论何种信用证，最后都有“付款”这个环节，所以将“honour”广译为“付款”更妥当。诚然，将“honour”译为“付款”，与将“payment”译为“付款”，应该是有区别的，笔者认为：前者的含义更加广阔，它不仅体现最后的“付款”环节，还包括“付款”前的环节，诸如“提示”、“付款承诺”及“承兑”等。正如本惯例第一条所指出那样，有的内容更适合在本惯例内解释。

4. 本条对“提示”作了解释。“提示”环节中的当事人是哪些呢？惯例列举了三个方面，即信用证的受益人、被指定银行及其他一方。前两方容易理解。例如受益人装运货物后，将货运单据或其他单据一并送交出口地银行办理押汇或者不押汇。出口地银行审核收到的单据后再将之送交付款行收款。因此，在通常情况下，做出提示的单位，应该是信用证的受益人、被指定的银行。至于“其他一方”是何方呢，笔者认为，是否可以考虑个别出证机构签发证书后，直接将有关证书送交银行。如一些地方的保险公司接受出口企业投保后，将缮制出的保险单据，直接送交出口地银行，在银行汇总成整套出口单据，向付款行收取货款。

[与第500号出版物比较]

本条中有不少新的内容。但也有部分内容，涉及第500出版物的第二、十四条等。

1.“相符提示”（complying presentation）是新的提法，指在符合信用证和惯例相关的规定，以及国际标准银行实务等三方面要求的情况下，（单据）才能作提示。而在第500号出版物中仅规定单据在“与信用证条款相符的条件下提示”。由此可见，在新条款中对提示的要求，较前更为严格，“提示”从符合一方面规定（信用证）到符合三方面规定。

2.本条将跟单信用证分成三种形式：即期付款信用证，承兑付款信用证和延期付款信用证。删去了议付信用证。笔者认为，这样的修改，无疑是很正确的。因为任何一种跟单信用证，根据开证人的意愿，在开出的信用证中，既可以允许议付，也可以不允许议付。反之，如开出的信用证允许议付（无论公开或限制议付），那么，无论这份信用证是即期/承兑/延期付款的信用证，只要受益人能够满足证内规定的条件，提交证内所要求的单据，银行都可以给办理议付手续。因此，如果把议付列为一种信用证的形式，显然是不恰当的。

[原文] Article 3　Interpretations

For the purpose of these rules:

Where applicable, words in the singular include the plural and in the plural include the singular.

A credit is irrevocable even if there is no indication to that effect.

A document may be signed by handwriting, facsimile signature, perforated signature, stamp, symbol or any other mechanical or electronic method of authentication.

A requirement for a document to be legalized, visaed, certified or similar will be satisfied by any signature, mark, stamp or label on the document which appears to satisfy that requirement.

Branches of a bank in different countries are considered to be separate banks.

Terms such as "first class", "well known", "qualified", "independent", "official", "competent" or "local" used to describe the issuer of a document allow any issuer except the beneficiary to issue that document.

Unless required to be used in a document, words such as "prompt", "immediately" or "as soon as possible" will be disregarded.

The expression "on or about" or similar will be interpreted as a stipulation that an event is to occur during a period of five calendar days before until five calendar days after the specified date, both start and end dates included.

The words "to", "until", "till", "from" and "between" when used to determine a period of shipment include the date or dates mentioned, and the words "before" and "after" exclude the date mentioned.

The words "from" and "after" when used to determine a maturity date exclude the date mentioned.

The terms "first half" and "second half" of a month shall be construed respectively as the 1st to the 15th and the 16th to the last day of the month, all dates inclusive.

The terms "beginning", "middle" and "end" of a month shall be construed respectively as the 1st to the 10th, the 11th to the 20th and the 21st to the last day of the month, all dates inclusive.

[译文] 第三条　释义

就本惯例而言：

在适用条款中，单词的单复数同义。

即使信用证中没有明示是不可撤销的，信用证也是如此。

单据可以手签，也可用签样印制、穿孔签字、盖章、符号表示方式签署或者其他任何机械或电子证实的方法签署。

当信用证含有要求使单据合法、签证单据、证明单据或对单据有类似要求的条件时，只要单据表面已满足上述条件，即可由在单据上签字、标注、盖章或标签来满足。

一家银行在不同国家设立的分支机构均视为另一家银行。

当使用诸如“第一流”、“著名”、“合格”、“独立”、“正式”、“有资格”、“当地”等词语描述单据出单人时，单据的出单人可以是除受益人以外的任何人。

除非信用证中坚持要求单据中使用，银行对使用诸如“迅速”、“立即”、“尽快”之类词语将不予置理。

“于或约于”或类似意义的词语将被解释为一项规定，按此规定，某项事件将在明确指定的日期前后 5 个日历日内发生，起讫日均包括在内。

当使用词语“止”、“至”、“直至”、“从”及“在……之间”确定装运期限时，应理解为包括所述日期。词语“……以前”和“……以后”，应理解为不包括所述日期。

当使用词语“从……”和“……后”确定到期日时应理解为不包括所述日期。

“上半月”和“下半月”应分别理解为自每月“1 日至 15 日”和“16 日至月末最后一天”，包括起讫日。

“月初”、“月中”和“月末”应分别理解为每月 1 日至 10 日、11 日至 20 日和 21 日至月末最后一天，包括起讫日。

[讲解]

1. 本条开始就指出：在本惯例内的各条款中，涉及有关词汇的单、复数，都包含着同样的含义。之所以提出这点，恐怕是考虑到不同文字的表达方式有所不同的关系。如惯例中当提到信用证的“当事人”、“议付单证”时，英文的词汇后加上“s”，表示是多数的，但翻译成中文后，当事人及单证不便突出是单或复数。所以本条首先明确单、复数都具有同样含义。

2. 本条首次指出：信用证是不可撤销的。这就结束半个多世纪以来对信用证形式的规定：可撤销的或不可撤销的。笔者认为，本条取消对信用证可以有“可撤销”的规定，具有双重意义：一方面加大开证行的责任感，另一方面增加受益人对信用证的信任，不再担心来证是否“可撤销”而存有疑虑。

3. 强调对提供单据的要求。只要单据使用诸如签字、注明或盖章等方式来达到单据合法、签证单据及证实单据的目的就可以。

4. 强调一家银行在不同国家设立的分支机构，当作为另一家银行来对待。从这点看，是充分考虑到银行（特别是开证行）的具体情况和利益的。例如，A 银行应开证人的请求，向 B 国的受益人 P 公司开出信用证。而 P 公司所在地也有 A 银行分行。当 P 公司将货物装运出口后，它可以持信用证内规定的单据，向当地 A 银行分行索取款项。如果 P 公司能达到在出口地全额收回货款的目的，无疑是非常有利的，这不仅大大地节省资金回收时间，加速资金周转，同时，如果所送的单据发生单单、单证（信用证）不相符时，P 公司还可以在出口地就地尽快解决。但是，这种情况无论对 A 银行或其在出口地分行显然是不利的。因为 A 银行在没有审核单据前，就要支付货款，而其分行未了解信用证的开证情况，仅收到单据后就支付货款，这样对两处银行非常不利。为此，惯例对两处银行的地位，作了明确规定。

［与第500号出版物比较］

本条在用词方面，有多处涉及第500号出版物的第二、六、二十及四十七条。

1. 本条取消了“可撤销信用证”的规定。今后信用证只有“不可撤销信用证”一种，这是一条重大的规定。

2. 在装运时间的规定上，除沿用原有的“止”（to）、“直至”（till）、“至”（until）等外，新增加“在……之间”（between）和“……之前”（before）。这是结合对装运日期的规定不断多样而设定的。如“8月15日前装运”（shipment before 15th Aug.），在理解和使用时，不应包括当天在内。“15日至25日之间装运”（shipment between 15th to 25th），则应理解为在15日至25日之间，包括当天在内装运是有效的。

3. 本条内有类似规定：“诸如‘第一流’、‘著名’……，单据的出单人可以是除受益人之外的任何人士”。原第500号出版物内有关规定是“不应使用诸如‘第一流’、‘著名’……，单据并非由受益人出具”。前者的规定比后者明确、肯定。

［原文］**Article 4　Credits v. Contracts**

a. A credit by its nature is a separate transaction from the sale or other contract on which it may be based. Banks are in no way concerned with or bound by such contract, even if any reference whatsoever to it is included in the credit. Consequently, the undertaking of a bank to honour, to negotiate or to fulfill any other obligation under the credit is not subject to claims or defences by the applicant resulting from its relationships with the issuing bank or the beneficiary.

A beneficiary can in no case avail itself of the contractual relationships existing between banks or between the applicant and the issuing bank.

b. An issuing bank should discourage any attempt by the applicant to include, as an integral part of the credit, copies of the underlying contract, proforma invoice and the like.

［译文］第四条　信用证与合同

a. 信用证就性质而言是独立于可能作为其依据的销售合同或其他合同的交易。即使信用证中涉及该合同，银行亦与该合同完全无关，且不受其约束。因此，一家银行做出付款、议付或履行信用证项下任何义务的承诺，并不受存在于由申请人与开证行之间或与受益人之间关系产生的索偿或抗辩的约束。

受益人在任何情况下，不得利用存在于银行之间或申请人与开证行之间的契约关系。

b. 开证行应劝阻申请人试图将基础合同、形式发票或其他类似文件的副本作为信用证整体组成部分的任何做法。

［讲解］

1. 本条再次重申信用证与合同的关系。特别强调两者都是独立的文件，即使在信用证中提到合同，银行也与该合同无关，也不受其约束。如有的来证，往往有“this L/C established per sales contract No.xxxx”等词句。虽有类似词句，银行也不会受该合同约束。在这种情况下，过去有的开证人就把合同副本、形式发票等类似文件作为信用证的附件，一并开给受益人。但本条已明确要求开证行劝阻这种做法。今后遇到一笔出口品种众多、规格及单价复杂的交易（如工艺品、金银饰品等）应如何制作单据呢？笔者认为，有的货物规格种类多，因而单价也多，如开证时将一系列单价都列在信用证上，极易发生差错，甚至会一再修改信用证，影响出运。在这种情况下，受益人只能根据出口合同内货物的多种规格、单价仔细制作单据。由于信用证内没有列明规格、单价，银行无法审核此项内容。因此，受益人应该加大对单据上有关内容的自我审核力度。

2. 对于装运日期的规定，本条加上“……之间”（between）和“……之前”（before）笔者认为，它更具有肯定的意思。如“shipment between 20th to 30th”，“Shipment before the end of Aug. 2005”。

3. 再次强调信用证的独立性。银行承担的付款、承兑汇票并付款以及议付货款的责任，不能也不会受到申请人和开证行之间、申请人和受益人之间已经产生有关偿付或其他方面联系的影响。

［与第500号出版物比较］

本条大部分内容引用第500号出版物的第三、五、四十七条。更动较大之处是：第500号出版物规定，开证行在开证时要尽量劝阻开证人引用原来开出的信用证及包括修改过的有关内容（在第500号惯例实施前常有这种做法），为了避免由于引用过多内容造成混乱，导致单据发生差错。本条扩大到开证时，开证行要尽量劝阻开证人不要将合同副本、形式发票等有关类似文件，作为新开出信用证的附件。两者的目的是一致的，都是为了避免差错，但本条比旧条文劝阻的范围扩大了。

［原文］Article 5　Documents v. Goods, Services or Performance

Banks deal with documents and not with goods, services or performance to which the documents may relate.

［译文］第五条　单据与货物/服务/行为

银行仅处理单据，而不是单据所涉及的货物、服务或其他行为。

[讲解]

本条再次强调银行处理的仅限于单据，决不涉及货物/服务/行为的内容（例如招标、投标或拍卖活动等）以及其他有关的行为（如履约的担保、借款担保等）。例如，一批货物装船后，船在航行中沉没，致使货物全部损失。但是，当提交给银行的单据，能够达到完全符合信用证的规定时，银行仍须支付款项。至于对遭受损失货物的赔偿，以及对货物损失善后处理等项问题，则由其他单位如保险公司来处理，与银行无关。

[与第 500 号出版物比较]

本条基本沿用第 500 号出版物的第四条内容，没有增添新的内容。但从第 500 号和第 600 号这两个出版物的都专项列出本条内容来看，说明惯例的制定者对于信用证只强调单据，而不涉及货物的重视程度。

[原文] **Article 6　Availability, Expiry Date and Place for Presentation**

a. A credit must state the bank with which it is available or whether it is available with any bank. A credit available with a nominated bank is also available with the issuing bank.

b. A credit must state whether it is available by sight payment, deferred payment, acceptance or negotiation.

c. A credit must not be issued available by a draft drawn on the applicant.

d. i. A credit must state an expiry date for presentation. An expiry date stated for honour or negotiation will be deemed to be an expiry date for presentation.

ii. The place of the bank with which the credit is available is the place for presentation. The place for presentation under a credit available with any bank is that of any bank. A place for presentation other than that of the issuing bank is in addition to the place of the issuing bank.

e. Except as provided in sub-article 29 (a), a presentation by or on behalf of the beneficiary must be made on or before the expiry date.

[译文] 第六条　适用性、有效期及提示地点

a. 信用证必须规定适用的银行，或者信用证是否对任何银行均适用。适用于指定银行的信用证同样也适用于开证行。

b. 信用证必须规定它是否适用于即期付款、延期付款、承兑抑或议付。

c. 不得开立包含有以申请人为汇票付款人条款的信用证。

d.i 信用证必须规定提示单据的有效期。信用证中规定的付款或者议付的有效期将被认为是提示单据的有效期限。

ii. 信用证适用的银行所在地就是提示单据的地点。对任何银行均适用的信用证项下单据所提示的地点是任何银行所在地。开证行所在地外的提示单据地点是除开证行所在地之外提交单据的地点。

e. 除非如29（a）中规定，由受益人或代表受益人提示的单据必须在到期日当日或在此之前提交。

[讲解]

1. 本条很强调信用证的“有效性”。因为，信用证一旦被开证行开出后，就要体现它是具有银行信用性质的书面文件，应该规定它的使用范围。是否所有的银行，还是部分银行可以使用它？否则，这些未被指定/被指定使用信用证的银行如果另外开出信用证，应该对原来的被使用信用证的开证行也同样也是有效的。

2. 本条对开证银行做了明确规定。要求开出的信用证要清楚规定：使用本证的银行是任何银行，还是有限的被指定的银行。

3. 本条对信用证方式下的当事人用什么方式取得款项，也做了明确规定，要求信用证内要规定本证的收款方式：即期付款或承兑付款或延期付款，还是允许受益人将单据办理押汇。

4. 本条对汇票上的付款人做了严格规定。最早在第 400 号出版物内规定，允许以开证人作为汇票的付款人。第 500 号出版物使用时，不允许以开证人作为付款人，付款人必须是开证行，这就实际加大开证行的责任感。但还允许以开证人作为付款人的汇票存在，银行只把它当作一般单据对待。而第 600 号出版物则不同，根本不允许开出以开证人作为付款人的汇票。

5. 本条规定，信用证应规定交单日期，如果证上仅规定付款或议付日期，也可以把它当作交单日对待。

6. 本条中也明确规定，凡使用该信用证的银行所在地点，即可以作为交付单据的地点。如证内指定上海某银行使用该信用证（如银行将该证递交受益人、银行对受益人办理押议付手续等），则该证的交单地也在上海。如证内对使用该证的银行未做规定时，那么，该证的使用地，也就是交单地。另外，如果证内规定在开证行以外的地点提示单据时，则交付单据时也应照此办理。

7. 本条强调除本出版物规定的某些特殊情况外，提示单据手续必须在信用证到期的当天或到期日之前办理。

[与第 500 号出版物比较]

本条涉及第 500 号出版物的第十、四十二及四十三条。

1. 本条新增加“有效性”，就是指开出的信用证要指明对哪个银行有效，还是对一切银行有效，开出的信用证可适用何种付款办法——即期付款、承兑付款、延期付款还是可以议付货款。而第 500 号出版物仅有议付信用证才被允许议付货款。

2. 信用证内提到“不允许”受益人开出以开证人为付款人的汇票。句中的语气是绝对的，用的是“必须不能”（must not），不像以前的几个出版物用的口气比较婉转“应该不能”（should

not）。

3. 本条新加一段关于信用证的使用地点和提示单据地点问题。强调信用证的使用地与提示单据地的一致性。如信用证在A地使用时，提示单据的地点也应在A地。

4. 本条与第500号出版物的第四十二条部分内容相似。但不像第500号出版物的第四十三条那样，规定交单日不能超过装运日期后21天。因为后面的条文对21天有更加明确、具体的规定。所以，本条就没有规定最迟交单日期。

［原文］**Article 7　Issuing Bank Undertaking**

a. Provided that the stipulated documents are presented to the nominated bank or to the issuing bank and that they constitute a complying presentation, the issuing bank must honour if the credit is available by:

i. sight payment, deferred payment or acceptance with the issuing bank;

ii. sight payment with a nominated bank and that nominated bank does not pay;

iii. deferred payment with a nominated bank and that nominated bank does not incur its deferred payment undertaking or, having incurred its deferred payment undertaking, does not pay at maturity;

iv. acceptance with a nominated bank and that nominated bank does not accept a draft drawn on it or, having accepted a draft drawn on it, does not pay at maturity;

v. negotiation with a nominated bank and that nominated bank does not negotiate.

b. An issuing bank is irrevocably bound to honour as of the time it issues the credit.

c. An issuing bank undertakes to reimburse a nominated bank that has honoured or negotiated a complying presentation and forwarded the documents to the issuing bank. Reimbursement for the amount of a complying presentation under a credit available by acceptance or deferred payment is due at maturity, whether or not the nominated bank prepaid or purchased before maturity. An issuing bank's undertaking to reimburse a nominated bank is independent of the issuing bank's undertaking to the beneficiary.

[译文] 第七条　开证行的承诺

a. 在规定的单据被提交至被指定银行或开证行并构成相符提示的情况下，如果信用证适用以下所列条款，开证行必须予以付款：

i. 应由开证行即期付款、延期付款或者承兑；

ii. 应由指定银行即期付款但被指定银行未予付款；

iii. 应由指定银行延期付款但指定银行未履行其延期付款承诺，或者虽已履行延期付款承诺但到期未予付款；

iv. 应由指定银行承兑但指定银行不予承兑以其为付款人的汇票，或者虽已承兑以其为付款人的汇票但到期未予付款；

v. 应由指定银行议付但被指定银行不予议付。

b. 从信用证开立之时起，开证行即有不可撤销的付款责任。

c. 但被指定银行对于单据相符提示已经付款或议付且这些单据已经寄往开证行的情况下，开证行有义务对被指定银行偿付。无论被指定银行是否于到期日前已经对相符提示予以预付或者包买，开证行对于承兑或延期付款信用证项下构成相符提示金额的偿付都应于到期日进行。开证行偿付被指定银行的承诺独立于开证行对于受益人的承诺。

[讲解]

1. 如果提交到开证行或指定银行的单据符合信用证要求时，开证行必须根据信用证适用于即期/承兑/延期付款的具体情况及时予以付款。

2. 如果被开证行指定执行即期/承兑并到期付款/延期付款以及议付单据的银行，没有按照开证行的指示去做，则开证行有责任继续自行履行上述义务。

3. 由于信用证只有不可撤销的信用证一种，所以，信用证开出后，就已经不可撤销地承担付款的责任。

4. 开证行保证做到：（1）对已经付款或议付，并已将正确单据寄往开证行索偿的被指定银行，偿付已经垫付的款项；（2）对远期的付款，无论所提交的单据是否已经获得预付款项，或者单据已被购买，开证行都保证对承兑信用证或延期付款信用证，到期偿付所提交单据上列明的款项。

［与第500号出版物比较］

本条涉及第500出版物的第九条部分内容。

1. 第500号出版物将开证行和保兑行的责任一并陈述，而在第600号出版物中，将开证行的承诺（也就是责任）与保兑行的承诺分两条各自陈述，由此可见对开证行的重视程度。此外，本条更加明确地规定开证行的责任。

2. 本条实际上是重申开证行对受益人以及有关指定银行负有第一性付款责任的承诺。

［原文］Article 8　Confirming Bank Undertaking

a. Provided that the stipulated documents are presented to the confirming bank or to any other nominated bank and that they constitute a complying presentation, the confirming bank must:

i. honour, if the credit is available by:

a) sight payment, deferred payment or acceptance with the confirming bank;

b) sight payment with another nominated bank and that nominated bank does not pay;

c) deferred payment with another nominated bank and that nominated bank does not incur its deferred payment undertaking or, having incurred its deferred payment undertaking, does not pay at maturity;

d) acceptance with another nominated bank and that nominated bank does not accept a draft drawn on it or, having accepted a draft drawn on it, does not pay at maturity;

e) negotiation with another nominated bank and that nominated bank does not negotiate.

ii. negotiate, without recourse, if the credit is available by negotiation with the confirming bank.

b. A confirming bank is irrevocably bound to honour or negotiate as of the time it adds its confirmation to the credit.

c. A confirming bank undertakes to reimburse another nominated bank that has honoured or negotiated a complying presentation and forwarded the documents to the confirming bank. Reimbursement for the amount of a complying presentation under a credit available by acceptance or deferred payment is due at maturity, whether or not another nominated bank prepaid or purchased before maturity. A confirming bank's undertaking to reimburse another nominated bank is independent of the confirming bank's undertaking to the beneficiary.

d. If a bank is authorized or requested by the issuing bank to confirm a credit but is not prepared to do so, it must inform the issuing bank without delay and may advise the credit without confirmation.

[译文] 第八条　保兑行的承诺

a. 如果规定的单据提交至保兑行或者其他被指定银行并构成相符提示，保兑行必须执行如下行为：

i. 付款，如果信用证适用于：

a）由保兑行即期付款、延期付款或者承兑；

b）由另一家被指定银行即期付款但被指定银行不予付款；

c）由另一家被指定银行延期付款但被指定银行未履行其延期付款的承诺，或者虽已履行延期付款承诺但到期不予付款；

d）由另一家被指定银行承兑但被指定银行不予承兑以其为付款人的汇票，或者虽已承兑以其为付款人的汇票但到期不予付款；

e）由另一家被指定银行议付而该被指定银行未予议付。

ii. 无追索权地议付，如果信用证适用于保兑行议付。

b. 从为信用证加具保兑之时起，保兑行即有不可撤销地付款或者议付责任。

c. 保兑行承诺在单据构成相符提示时已予以付款或者议付并将单据寄往开证行的另一家被指定银行进行偿付。无论另一家被指定银行是否在到期日前已经对相符提示项下信用证予以预付或者包买，保兑行对于承兑或延期付款信用证项下构成相符提示金额的偿付都应于到期日进行。保兑行偿付另一家被指定银行的承诺独立于保兑行对受益人的承诺。

d. 如开证行授权或要求另一家银行对信用证加具保兑，而该银行不准备照办时，它必须毫不延误地告知开证行，同时可以不加保兑并将此份未经保兑的信用证通知受益人。

[讲解]

对于保兑行来说，它承担的责任与上条对开证行应承担的责任基本一致，说明开证行与保兑行都承担第一性付款责任，绝不是开证行（付款行）履行不了其付款责任时，才由保兑行承担起付款的责任。但是，在本条中也指出两家银行还是存在一些比较重要区别的：如当保兑行被指定为议付行时，保兑行的议付是没有追索权的。

[与第 500 号出版物比较]

本条涉及第 500 号出版物的第九条。原来将开证行和保兑行两者合在一条，新的出版物将两家承担责任基本相同的银行，分开两条规定各自的责任，由此可见惯例制定者对这两家银行的重视程度。

[原文] Article 9 Advising of Credits and Amendments

a. A credit and any amendment may be advised to a beneficiary through an advising bank. An advising bank that is not a confirming bank advises the credit and any amendment without any undertaking to honour or negotiate.

b. By advising the credit or amendment, the advising bank signifies that it has satisfied itself as to the apparent authenticity of the credit or amendment and that the advice accurately reflects the terms and conditions of the credit or amendment received.

c. An advising bank may utilize the services of another bank ("second advising bank") to advise the credit and any amendment to the beneficiary. By advising the credit or amendment, the second advising bank signifies that it has satisfied itself as to the apparent authenticity of the advice it has received and that the advice accurately reflects the terms and conditions of the credit or amendment received.

d. A bank utilizing the services of an advising bank or second advising bank to advise a credit must use the same bank to advise any amendment thereto.

e. If a bank is requested to advise a credit or amendment but elects not to do so, it must so inform, without delay, the bank from which the credit, amendment or advice has been received.

f. If a bank is requested to advise a credit or amendment but cannot satisfy itself as to the apparent authenticity of the credit, the amendment or the advice, it must so inform, without delay, the bank from which the instructions appear to have been received. If the advising bank or second advising bank elects nonetheless to advise the credit or amendment, it must inform the beneficiary or second advising bank that it has not been able to satisfy itself as to the apparent authenticity of the credit, the amendment or the advice.

[译文] 第九条　关于信用证及修改的通知

a. 信用证及其修改可以通过通知行通知受益人。如果通知行不是保兑行，信用证通知行对所通知的信用证不承诺付款或议付。

b. 信用证或其修改的通知标志着通知行认为信用证或其修改的表面真实性得到满足，并且该通知准确地反映了所收到的信用证或信用证修改的条款。

c. 通知行可以使用另一家银行的服务（“第二通知行”）来通知受益人其信用证和信用证的任何修改。信用证或其修改的通知标志着第二通知行认为信用证或其修改的表面真实性得到满足，并且该通知准确地反映了所收到的信用证或信用证修改的条款。

d. 无论银行使用通知行还是第二通知行的服务来通知受益人，其信用证都必须使用同一家银行的服务来通知此信用证的修改。

e. 如果银行决定不予通知其被要求通知的信用证或信用证修改，它必须毫不延误地告知向其发送信用证、修改或通知的银行。

f. 如果被要求通知信用证或信用证修改的银行不能确定信用证、修改或通知的表面真实性，它就必须毫不延误地告知向其发送该指示的银行。如果通知行或第二通知行仍决定通知该信用证或信用证修改，则必须告知受益人或第二通知行其未能核实信用证、修改或通知的表面真实性。

[讲解]

1. 本条对通知行的责任做了较明确的规定，即通知行除非也是保兑行，否则不必承担承兑和议付货款的责任。但通知行在履行其通知义务时，至少要掌握信用证及修改表上看来是真实的。

2. 如果不是通知行自己而由另一家银行（第二通知行）将收到的信用证去通知受益人，这种情况是允许的。第二通知行的权利和义务与通知行相同。

3. 如果开证行选定一家银行作为通知行时，必须始终利用该通知行的服务。例如，A 银行开立一张信用证，通过 B 银行将该信用证传递给 Y 公司，以后凡有关该证的修改等事项，A 银行必须继续利用 B 银行的服务，将有关该证的修改等事项，传递给 Y 公司，不得更换通知银行。

4. 如果通知行不打算将收到的信用证或修改通知受益人/第二通知行，或不能确定收到的信用证/修改/通知是否真实时，它必须将它的决定/怀疑，毫不延迟地告知原发送银行。如果通知行仍愿履行它的通知职责，它也必须把它认为的疑点，告知受益人/第二通知行，以便让当事人知情和酌情处理。

[与第 500 号出版物比较]

本条涉及第 500 号出版物的第七、十一条。在银行业务的实践过程，不少信用证是通过第二通知行传递给受益人的，但在第 500 号出版物中，对此并未做出相关规定。第 600 号出版物对此进行了确认。

［原文］**Article 10　Amendments**

a. Except as otherwise provided by article 38, a credit can neither be amended nor cancelled without the agreement of the issuing bank, the confirming bank, if any, and the beneficiary.

b. An issuing bank is irrevocably bound by an amendment as of the time it issues the amendment. A confirming bank may extend its confirmation to an amendment and will be irrevocably bound as of the time it advises the amendment. A confirming bank may, however, choose to advise an amendment without extending its confirmation and, if so, it must inform the issuing bank without delay and inform the beneficiary in its advice.

c. The terms and conditions of the original credit (or a credit incorporating previously accepted amendments) will remain in force for the beneficiary until the beneficiary communicates its acceptance of the amendment to the bank that advised such amendment. The beneficiary should give notification of acceptance or rejection of an amendment. If the beneficiary fails to give such notification, a presentation that complies with the credit and to any not yet accepted amendment will be deemed to be notification of acceptance by the beneficiary of such amendment. As of that moment the credit will be amended.

d. A bank that advises an amendment should inform the bank from which it received the amendment of any notification of acceptance or rejection.

e. Partial acceptance of an amendment is not allowed and will be deemed to be notification of rejection of the amendment.

f. A provision in an amendment to the effect that the amendment shall enter into force unless rejected by the beneficiary within a certain time shall be disregarded.

[译文] 第十条 信用证的修改

a. 除第三十八条另有规定外，未经开证行、保兑行（如有），以及受益人同意，信用证既不能修改也不能撤销。

b. 自发出信用证修改之时起，开证行就不可撤销地受其所发出修改的约束。保兑行可将其保兑承诺扩展至修改，且自其通知该修改之时起，即不可撤销地受到修改的约束。然而，保兑行可选择仅将修改通知受益人而不对其加具保兑，但必须毫不延误地将此通知开证行和受益人。

c. 在受益人向通知修改的银行表示接受该修改内容之前，原信用证（或先前已经修改过的信用证）的条款对受益人仍然有效。受益人应告知向其通知修改的银行是接受或拒绝接受修改。如受益人未发出上述通知，当其提交给指定银行或开证行的单据与信用证以及尚未表示接受的修改的要求一致时，则该事实即视为受益人已做出接受修改的通知，并从此时起，该信用证已做修改。

d. 通知信用证修改的银行应当告知向其发出修改通知的银行任何有关接受或拒绝接受该修改的通知。

e. 接受部分修改内容是不允许的，并且将被认为拒绝接受修改的通知。

f. 信用证修改的内容中关于除非受益人在某一时间段内拒绝接受修改，否则该修改将开始生效的条款将被不予置理。

[讲解]

1. 由于信用证的特点决定，信用证开出后，未经受益人和有关方面同意（有关方面主要指开证行、偿付行及保兑行等），不得单方面修改信用证内容或撤销信用证（第 600 号出版物已经明确凡跟单信用证都是“不可撤销”的）。

2. 开证行修改证内的内容后，就自然接受修改后内容的约束。同样，保兑行也就将其保兑的责任，延展到所修改的内容。但是，保兑行可以将修改不加保兑地转交给受益人，如果保兑行这样做时，它应该毫不迟延地通知开证行和受益人。这点充分体现开证行和保兑行在对待信用证的修改上，在做法方面的重要区别。

3. 当受益人收到修改后，要表示接受还是拒绝接受修改内容。作为通知行，应当及时把受益人的表态告知开证行。受益人在未表态之前，仍受原证 / 原先已作过修改的信用证的约束。如果受益人在送交单据时，所提交的单据和经修改内容一致，那么，事实上说明受益人已接受修改，也表示受益人做出了接受修改的通知。如果提交的单据与修改内容不一致，而与修改前的内容相符时，则也可以说明这是受益人做出了拒绝接受修改的通知。

例如，某信用证货物数量为100吨，其装、效期均为7月31日，受益人担心装、效期时间过短，租船订舱有困难，要求开证人将装、效期延展至8月5日。后来，开证人虽修改了装、效日，但同时却将数量减至80吨。受益人备齐货后，8月4日将80吨货物的单据送交银行，这就意味受益人用行动表示接受修改。如果受益人不愿接受减少出运货物的修改，经过努力，在7月31日将100吨货物装运，并于当天将100吨货物的全套正确单据送交银行，这就意味受益人用行动表示拒绝接受修改，这样做也是可以的。

4. 对修改的内容，要么全部接受，要么全部拒绝。不允许接受部分内容而拒绝另一部分内容。如在上例中，受益人要求开证人延展装、效期，开证人在修改的通知中，不仅延展了装、效期，并且还主动减少了原证内要求装运的数量，即从100吨降到80吨（可能国外市场上对该种货物需求疲软，市价下跌）。受益人对这样的修改，要么全部接受，要么完全拒绝，不能仅接受延展装、效期而拒绝装运数量减少的修改。

5. 本条指出，受益人对信用证的修改要用行动明白表态，是接受还是拒绝接受修改。如上例所述，受益人在 7 月 31 日交付装运 100 吨货物的单据，或在 8 月 4 日交付装运 80 吨货物的单据，用这样的行动来表示拒绝 / 接受修改)，不允许以“默示”方式来表达自己的态度，如 8 月 4 日交付装运 100 吨货物的单据，这样做是不允许的。

[与第 500 号出版物比较]

本条主要涉及第 500 号出版物的第九条。

1. 在第 500 号出版物中，有关信用证修改事宜，只作为第九条的部分内容。但在实际业务中，一份信用证开出后，修改证内内容的情况经常出现。第 600 号出版物单独列出本条，并且较详细地规定有关修改事宜，这无疑是很必要的。

2. 信用证在修改过程中，还常出现一些问题和争议。本条用 6 点分别列出有关方面的职责，比较明确地分清有关当事者的责任。

[原文] Article 11 Teletransmitted and Pre-Advised Credits and Amendments

a. An authenticated teletransmission of a credit or amendment will be deemed to be the operative credit or amendment, and any subsequent mail confirmation shall be disregarded.

If a teletransmission states “full details to follow” (or words of similar effect), or states that the mail confirmation is to be the operative credit or amendment, then the teletransmission will not be deemed to be the operative credit or amendment. The issuing bank must then issue the operative credit or amendment without delay in terms not inconsistent with the teletransmission.

b. A preliminary advice of the issuance of a credit or amendment (“pre-advice”) shall only be sent if the issuing bank is prepared to issue the operative credit or amendment. An issuing bank that sends a pre-advice is irrevocably committed to issue the operative credit or amendment, without delay, in terms not inconsistent with the pre-advice.

[译文] 第十一条　电讯传递与预先通知的信用证及其修改

a. 经证实的信用证或其修改的电讯指示即被认为是有效的信用证或其修改的文件，且将对任何随后邮寄的证实书不予置理。

若该电讯声明“详情后告”（或类似词语）或声明邮寄的证实书将是有效的信用证或信用证修改，则该电讯将被认为是无效的信用证或修改。开证行必须毫不延误地开出有效的信用证或修改，且该信用证条款不能与电讯内容相矛盾。

b. 唯有准备开立有效信用证或修改的开证行，才可以对有效信用证或修改发送预先通知书。发出预先通知的开证行应不可撤销地保证不延误地开出有效的信用证或修改，且该信用证条款不能与预先通知书相矛盾。

[讲解]

1. 本条指出用电讯方式传递信用证和其修改的效力问题。过去，开证行用电讯方式开出的信用证后，往往还要将信用证正本邮寄给受益人作为证实。在第500号出版物中对此已有规定：如果电开信用证的内容完备有效，无须再加证实。如果开证行还要发出证实书，那么，这个证实书可视作无效，以免在制单等环节中无所依循。第600号出版物也有类似内容，但语气更强、更肯定。

2. 本条对“预先通知”和“详情后告”的信用证和修改，和第500号出版物一样，都有说明，但第600号出版物中的提法更加肯定。

[与第 500 号出版物比较]

本条内容与第 500 出版物的第十一条基本相同，但语气更强。

[原文] Article 12　Nomination

a. Unless a nominated bank is the confirming bank, an authorization to honour or negotiate does not impose any obligation on that nominated bank to honour or negotiate, except when expressly agreed to by that nominated bank and so communicated to the beneficiary.

b. By nominating a bank to accept a draft or incur a deferred payment undertaking, an issuing bank authorizes that nominated bank to prepay or purchase a draft accepted or a deferred payment undertaking incurred by that nominated bank.

c. Receipt or examination and forwarding of documents by a nominated bank that is not a confirming bank does not make that nominated bank liable to honour or negotiate, nor does it constitute honour or negotiation.

[译文] 第十二条　指定

a. 除非指定银行是保兑行，对指定银行付款或议付的授权并不能强制指定银行履行付款或议付的义务，但指定银行已明确同意并照此告知受益人的情形除外。

b. 当指定一家银行承兑汇票或做出延期付款承诺时，开证行即授权该指定银行预付或包买经该银行承兑的汇票或由该银行做出延期付款的承诺。

c. 非保兑行的指定银行接受、审核并寄送单据的行为既不能使该指定银行具有付款或议付的责任，也不构成该银行的付款或议付。

［讲解］

1. 本条明确指定银行的独主性。一家银行作为指定银行后，它可以明确表示同意/不同意执行付款和议付的指示。

2. 本条也明确指出，如果开证行指定一家银行具有承兑汇票（远期付款）或开出延期付款承诺（延期付款）的权力。开证银行就同样授予该行具有付款、贴现经其承兑后的汇票和延期付款承诺到期付款的权力。

3. 如果一家被指定银行但并非保兑银行，它虽具有审核单据和寄交单据责任，但并不具有付款和议付的义务。

［与第500号出版物比较］

1. 本条与第500号出版物的第十八条中某些内容相似，但本条更加强调被指示银行的独立性。即对于开证行的一些指示，被指示银行既可以执行，也可以拒绝执行。

2. 第500号出版物内涉及一些费用由何方承担的问题。第600号出版物的未涉及这方面内容。总的来说，开证行应该承担经其发出指示在执行过程中产生的费用。

［原文］**Article 13　Bank-to-Bank Reimbursement Arrangements**

a. If a credit states that reimbursement is to be obtained by a nominated bank（"claiming bank"）claiming on another party（"reimbursing bank"）, the credit must state if the reimbursement is subject to the ICC rules for bank-to-bank reimbursements in effect on the date of issuance of the credit.

b. If a credit does not state that reimbursement is subject to the ICC rules for bank-to-bank reimbursements, the following apply:

i. An issuing bank must provide a reimbursing bank with a reimbursement authorization that conforms with the availability stated in the credit. The reimbursement authorization should not be subject to an expiry date.

ii. A claiming bank shall not be required to supply a reimbursing bank with a certificate of compliance with the terms and conditions of the credit.

iii. An issuing bank will be responsible for any loss of interest, together with any expenses incurred, if reimbursement is not provided on first demand by a reimbursing bank in accordance with the terms and conditions of the credit.

iv. A reimbursing bank's charges are for the account of the issuing bank. However, if the charges are for the account of the beneficiary, it is the responsibility of an issuing bank to indicate in the credit and in the reimbursement authorization. If a reimbursing bank's charges are for the account of the beneficiary, they shall be deducted from the amount due to a claiming bank when reimbursement is made. If no reimbursement is made, the reimbursing bank's charges remain the obligation of the issuing bank.

c. An issuing bank is not relieved of any of its obligations to provide reimbursement if reimbursement is not made by a reimbursing bank on first demand.

[译文] 第十三条　银行间的偿付约定

a. 倘若信用证规定偿付是通过指定银行（“索偿行”）向另一方银行（“偿付行”）索偿的方式取得，则信用证中必须规定是否从信用证开立生效日起适用于国际商会关于银行间偿付的统一规则。

b. 如果信用证中未声明是否适用于国际商会关于银行间偿付统一规则，则遵照于下列条款办理：

i. 开证行必须向偿付行提供偿付授权书，该授权书须与信用证中规定的有效条款相符。偿付授权书不应规定有效期。

ii. 不应要求索偿行向偿付行提供表明单据与信用证条款相符的证明书。

iii. 如果偿付行未能在根据信用证条款首次索偿时即行偿付，则开证行应对索偿行利息损失以及由此产生的费用负责。

iv. 偿付行的费用由开证行承担。然而，如果费用要由受益人承担，则开证行有责任在信用证和偿付授权书中予以注明。如偿付行的费用要由受益人承担，则该费用在偿付时从支付索偿行的总金额中扣除。如果未发生偿付，开证行仍有义务承担偿付行的费用。

c. 如果偿付行未能于索偿行首次索偿时即行偿付，那么开证行不能解除其自身的偿付责任。

[讲解]

1. 本条主要是说明银行之间在偿付方面责任的划分、费用的承担和办理有关事务的依据。

2. 本条明确在正常情况下，偿付行的费用由开证行支付，解决了偿付行在付款给受益人时往往自行扣除费用这个长期存在的问题。

3. 本条再次明确偿付行与信用证内规定各单据的关系。如果偿付行已经遵照开证行的通知，向受益人支付了款项，将来开证行收到的单据与信用证要求不相符时，偿付行不承担责任。

[与第500号出版物比较]

本条主要涉及第500号出版物的第十九条，但在一些内容方面，做了更明确的规定。例如，偿付行未能在第一次索偿时支付款项，第500号出版物规定开证行除要付款外，还要向索偿方加补利息损失。而第600号出版物则规定除要付款和加补利息外，还要对由此而产生的费用负责。

[原文] Article 14 Standard for Examination of Documents

a. A nominated bank acting on its nomination, a confirming bank, if any, and the issuing bank must examine a presentation to determine, on the basis of the documents alone, whether or not the documents appear on their face to constitute a complying presentation.

b. A nominated bank acting on its nomination, a confirming bank, if any, and the issuing bank shall each have a maximum of five banking days following the day of presentation to determine if a presentation is complying. This period is not curtailed or otherwise affected by the occurrence on or after the date of presentation of any expiry date or last day for presentation.

c. A presentation including one or more original transport documents subject to articles 19, 20, 21, 22, 23, 24 or 25 must be made by or on behalf of the beneficiary not later than 21 calendar days after the date of shipment as described in these rules, but in any event not later than the expiry date of the credit.

d. Data in a document, when read in context with the credit, the document itself and international standard banking practice, need not be identical to, but must not conflict with, data in that document, any other stipulated document or the credit.

e. In documents other than the commercial invoice, the description of the goods, services or performance, if stated, may be in general terms not conflicting with their description in the credit.

f. If a credit requires presentation of a document other than a transport document, insurance document or commercial invoice, without stipulating by whom the document is to be issued or its data content, banks will accept the document as presented if its content appears to fulfil the function of the required document and otherwise complies with sub-article

14 (d).

g. A document presented but not required by the credit will be disregarded and may be returned to the presenter.

h. If a credit contains a condition without stipulating the document to indicate compliance with the condition, banks will deem such condition as not stated and will disregard it.

i. A document may be dated prior to the issuance date of the credit, but must not be dated later than its date of presentation.

j. When the addresses of the beneficiary and the applicant appear in any stipulated document, they need not be the same as those stated in the credit or in any other stipulated document, but must be within the same country as the respective addresses mentioned in the credit. Contact details (telefax, telephone, E-mail and the like) stated as part of the beneficiary's and the applicant's address will be disregarded. However, when the address and contact details of the applicant appear as part of the consignee or notify party details on a transport document subject to articles 19, 20, 21, 22, 23, 24 or 25, they must be as stated in the credit.

k. The shipper or consignor of the goods indicated on any document need not be the beneficiary of the credit.

l. A transport document may be issued by any party other than a carrier, owner, master or charterer provided that the transport document meets the requirements of articles 19, 20, 21, 22, 23 or 24 of these rules.

[译文] 第十四条　审核单据的标准

a. 按照指定行事的指定银行、保兑行（如有），以及开证行必须仅以单据为基础对提示的单据进行审核，并且以此决定单据是否在表面上与信用证条款构成相符提示。

b. 按照指定行事的指定银行、保兑行（如有），以及开证行各自拥有从其收到提示单据的翌日起最多不超过 5 个银行工作日的时间以决定提示是否构成相符。该期限不因单据适逢提示有效期或者最迟提示期当日及其之后而被缩减或受到其他影响。

c. 提示若包含一份或多份按照本惯例第十九条、二十条、二十一条、二十二条、二十三条、二十四条或二十五条出具的正本运输单据，则必须由受益人或其代表按照上述条款在不迟于装运日后的 21 个日历日内提交，但无论如何提交不得迟于信用证的到期日。

d. 单据中内容不必与信用证、该项单据本身以及国际标准银行实务完全一致。但该项单据中的内容之间，或单据中内容与其他规定的单据或信用证不得互相冲突。

e. 除商业发票外，如果其他单据中有关货物、服务或行为描述须明示，可使用统称，但不得与信用证中的描述相矛盾。

f. 如果信用证中要求提交除运输单据、保险单据和商业发票以外的其他单据，且并未规定该单据由何人出具或单据的内容。只要所提交单据的内容看来满足其功能需要且其他方面与十四条（d）款相符，银行将对上述单据予以接受。

g. 对提交的单据中不是信用证中要求的，银行将不予置理，并且可以退还提示人。

h. 如果信用证中包含某项条件而未规定与之相符的提示单据，银行将认为信用证中未列明此条件，并对此不予置理。

i. 单据的出单日期可以早于信用证开立日期，但不得迟于信用证规定的提示日期。

j. 当受益人和申请人的地址显示在任何规定的单据上时，这些地址不必与信用证或其他规定单据中显示的地址相同，但必须分别与信用证中所述地址处于同一国家内。详细联系方式（电传、电话、电子邮箱及类似方式）如作为受益人和申请人地址的组成部分，银行对此将不予置理。然而，当申请人的地址及详细联系方式作为按照第十九条、二十条、二十一条、二十二条、二十三条、二十四条或二十五条出具的运输单据中收货人或通知方详细情况的组成部分时，则这些地址必须按照信用证规定予以显示。

k. 在任何单据中述及的货物托运人或发货人不必是信用证的受益人。

l. 如果运输单据能够满足本惯例第十九条、二十条、二十一条、二十二条、二十三条或二十四条的要求，则运输单据可以由除承运人、船东、船长或租船人外的任何一方出具。

［讲解］

1. 在信用证支付方式下，如何理解并做到单证（信用证）、单单一致，是一个很重要的问题。如何掌握过“活”，会违反信用证规定，收不回货款。但如果掌握过“死”，同样也会不符合信用证及惯例的规定，不仅可能收不回货款，甚至贻笑大方。如何做到真正理解单证一致、单单一致的含义？笔者认为，应该从以下关于单证一致、单单一致原则的解释来做具体分析。

（1）单据与信用证内条款表面完全一致的原则。指由受益人提供的单据所显示出来的内容，有一部分必须和信用证的规定完全一致。如公司名称为 ABC Co., Ltd. 既不能写成 abcco., ltd. 也不能写成 ABC CO., LTD. 否则，就可能被认为单证不一致。因为，这样做等于把对方的“大号”给改了，如果对方强调“单证不符”，也是有理由的。

（2）单据与信用证内条款对应一致的原则。指受益人提供单据的内容，除单据之间要一致外，也必须符合信用证的要求。如国外来证规定需要受益人提供“由专家签发的品质证明书”(Cert. of quality must be given by experts)。装运后，受益人提供有一位专家签字的品质证明书，结果遭到银行拒付。拒付的理由是来证规定要一位以上专家“experts”，而提供的证书只有一位专家签字，显然是单证不符。又如来证有以下规定：唛头如下：

B B S

HAMBURG

No.1—up

出口装运时，共 200 个纸箱，如果单据上仍照来证规定，照办写上 1—up，结果当然会造成银行拒付。有时制作单据人员不明白银行拒付的原因。关键是来证不知道货物将来要装多少箱或多少包，所以只写上 No.1—up，“up”是“起”的意思。而装运时已有了具体包装的数量。所以，单据上应写成 No.1—200。如果还照来证上所写生搬硬套，显然是不行的。

（3）单据与信用证条款逻辑一致的原则。如 CIF 贸易术语规定卖方投保、支付保险费并提供保险单据。同时，还要提供检验货物的品质证书及其他有关证书。在诸多证书中，保险单的日期，必须在签发提单日之前，这是为了表示货物是在装船前投保，符合保险责任起讫“仓至仓”条款的要求。同样，检验证书的检验日期，也应该在装船前，表示货物是在装船前报请检验的(极个别货物的投保和检验除外)。至于其他单据的出单日期，根据实际情况，可以有前有后，这就是逻辑一致的原则。

（4）单据与信用证条款含义一致的原则。例如，一份来证规定货物采用海运，CIF 贸易术语，货物自天津新港运到维也纳(奥地利）“From Xingang of Tianjin to Vienna”。这种规定显然不对，因为奥地利的维也纳在内陆，不能用 CIF 这个纯海运的贸易术语。如果货物确实要求运到维也纳，应该改用 CIP 贸易术语为宜。因为一般在这种情况下，要先用海运方式从天津新港将货物运到德国的港口，如汉堡港，再由汉堡用陆运方式将货物运至维也纳。所以，同样货物的 CIF 和 CIP 的单价自然不同。后者的承运人由于负责将货物运到目的地，付出的运输等费用比前者相对要高，因而转向托运人收取的费用也就相应提高。另外，由于这笔业务的整个运输过程不仅只是一种运输方式，所以使用的海运单据，就不应该使用直达 /转船提单（Direct/Transhipment Bill of

Lading)，而应该使用联运提单（Through Bill of Lading)。

2. 本条把银行工作日从7天缩减为5天，这显然考虑到受益人对加速资金回收的要求，对受益人无疑是非常有利的。

3. 本条明确规定，除运输单据、保险单据和商业发票外，对其他单据的出具人不做规定。这就使受益人制作单据时，得到极大便利。例如，信用证内规定要提供包装单（packing list)。受益人提供的包装单，既可由生产厂家制作，甚至也可由受益人以出口企业的身份自行制作。

4. 关于单据的出单日期问题，本条允许单据的出单日期早于信用证的开立日。也就是货物出运在前，出口成交在后。过去虽有类似规定，但往往前面还列有“除非信用证另有规定……”，本条则取消了类似词句，说明第600号出版物的制定者对这方面是很重视的，也是适当地考虑信用证受益人（卖方）的利益。这种做法是指，货物在成交前装上运输工具，向目标市场运去。在此同时，卖方也在积极寻找买主，如果成交，卖方所提交单据的日期（特别提单、保险单等主要单据）必然会早于信用证开证日。如果卖方找不到适合的买方，运出的货物不能在运输途中售出，则待货运到目的地后，由受卖方委托的代理人代替卖方提货、存仓和出售。这种“卖路货”的销售方式，对于一些竞争激烈的商品，为争夺市场，具有一定积极意义。本条的相应规定，可以说是配合这种交易方式而设定的。

5. 本条明确规定：显示在“任何”单据中的货物托运人或发货人，不必是信用证的受益人。这个规定，显然对使用“背对背信用证”十分有利。例如S公司是中间商，它不满足仅获得较少佣金作为自身的收益。佣金虽是中间商主要收入来源，但它并不能保证中间商能在较长时间获得它。因为当买方和供货商双方熟悉后，买方就不再依靠中间商S公司。如果S公司打算在较长时间内获得买卖货物的差价，而这种差价通常会高于佣金，便可以考虑使用“背对背信用证”。具体做法是：当S公司与国外买方 M 公司签订售货合同后，转向供货商购买同等规格数量的货物，但单价比售予 M 公司为低。S 公司借此赚取一买一卖之间的差价。S 公司在收到国外买方开来的信用证后，就以此证为基础，向供货商开出同样商品、同样规格数量但价格低于前者的信用证。为了对国外 M 公司“保密”，S 公司在开立给供货商的信用证内，指定一些单据（运输单据、检验单据等）上的发货人、检验申请人不是新开信用证上的受益人（即供货商）而是第三方，如运输承运人等。这样做就使得 M 公司从运输、检验等单据上找不到真正的供货人。M 公司在一定时期内，为购买货物而不得不通过中间商 S 公司，这就保障了 S 公司能较长期获得货物差价。本条规定，使得这样的做法更加“名正言顺”了。

[与第 500 号出版物比较]

本条在多处沿用第 500 号出版物的相关规定。如第十三、二十一、二十二、三十一、三十三、三十七和四十三条等。新的规定是：将银行审核单据的时间，从 7 个工作日压缩到 5 个工作日，使受益人“受益”。本条也对交单时间做了严格规定：在信用证的有效期日内，不得超过装运日后 21 天。再者，第 500 号出版物仅规定提单允许以受益人以外的一方为发货人，本条规定：任何单据都可以将受益人以外的一方为发货人。

[原文] Article 15　Complying Presentation

a. When an issuing bank determines that a presentation is complying, it must honour.

b. When a confirming bank determines that a presentation is complying, it must honour or negotiate and forward the documents to the issuing bank.

c. When a nominated bank determines that a presentation is complying and honours or negotiates, it must forward the documents to the confirming bank or issuing bank.

[译文] 第十五条　相符提示

a. 当开证行确定单据提示相符时，就必须予以付款。

b. 当保兑行确定单据提示相符时，就必须予以付款或议付，同时将单据寄往开证行。

c. 当指定银行确定单据提示相符并予以付款或议付时，必须将单据寄往保兑行或开证行。

[讲解]

本条是单独列出的，目的在于进一步明确开证行、保兑行和被指定银行的职责。“相符提示”的含义是：提交到开证行、保兑行和指定银行的单据，必须和信用证内要求和规定一致，才能获得相应的款项。

开证行、保兑行和指定银行确定送交的单据相符提示时。三家银行的做法是不相同的。

开证行——付款。

保兑行——付款/议付，并将经过审核正确的单据寄送开证行。

指定银行——付款/议付，并将经过审核正确的单据寄送保兑行/开证行。

[与第500号出版物比较]

本条与第500号出版物内相关内容相本相同，只是单列“相符提示”这条。

[原文] Article 16　Discrepant Documents, Waiver and Notice

a. When a nominated bank acting on its nomination, a confirming bank, if any, or the issuing bank determines that a presentation does not comply, it may refuse to honour or negotiate.

b. When an issuing bank determines that a presentation does not comply, it may in its sole judgement approach the applicant for a waiver of the discrepancies. This does not, however, extend the period mentioned in sub-article 14 (b).

c. When a nominated bank acting on its nomination, a confirming bank, if any, or the issuing bank decides to refuse to honour or negotiate, it must give a single notice to that effect to the presenter.

The notice must state:

i. that the bank is refusing to honour or negotiate; and

ii. each discrepancy in respect of which the bank refuses to honour or negotiate; and

iii. a) that thc bank is holding the documents pending further instructions from the presenter; or

b) that the issuing bank is holding the documents until it receives a waiver from the applicant and agrees to accept it, or receives further instructions from the presenter prior to agreeing to accept a waiver; or

c) that the bank is returning the documents; or

d) that the bank is acting in accordance with instructions previously received from the presenter.

d. The notice required in sub-article 16 (c) must be given by telecommunication or, if that is not possible, by other expeditious means no later than the close of the fifth banking day following the day of presentation.

e. A nominated bank acting on its nomination, a confirming bank, if any, or the issuing bank may, after providing notice required by sub-article 16 (c) (iii) (a) or (b), return the documents to the presenter at any time.

f. If an issuing bank or a confirming bank fails to act in accordance with the provisions of this article, it shall be precluded from claiming that the documents do not constitute a complying presentation.

g. When an issuing bank refuses to honour or a confirming bank refuses to honour or negotiate and has given notice to that effect in accordance with this article, it shall then be entitled to claim a refund, with interest, of any reimbursement made.

[译文] 第十六条　存在不符点的单据、不符点的放弃及不符点通知

a. 当按照指定行事的指定银行、保兑行（如有）或开证行确定提示不构成相符时，可以拒绝付款或议付。

b. 当开证行确定提示不构成相符时，可以依据其独立的判断建议申请人放弃有关不符点。然而，这并不因此延长第十四条（b）款中述及的期限。

c. 当按照指定行事的被指定银行、保兑行（如有）或开证行决定拒绝付款或议付时，必须单独发送含有此内容的通知给提示人。

通知必须声明：

i. 银行拒绝付款或议付；及

ii. 银行凭以拒绝付款或议付的各个不符点；及

iii. a）银行持有单据等待提示人进一步指示；或

b）开证行持有单据直至收到申请人的不符点放弃通知且同意接受该弃权，或开证行在同意接受弃权前从提示人处收到进一步指示；或

c）银行退回单据；或

d）银行根据以前从提示人处收到的指示行事。

d. 按第十六条（c）款中要求发出的通知必须以电讯方式发出，或者，如果不可能以电讯方式通知时，则须在不迟于提示单据日翌日起算第 5 个银行工作日结束前以其他快捷方式通知。

e. 按照指定行事的指定银行、保兑行（如有）或开证行，可以在提供第十六条（c）款（iii）、（a）或（b）款要求的通知后，在任何时间将单据退还提示人。

f. 如果开证行或保兑行未能按照本条款的规定行事，将无权宣称单据不构成相符提示。

g. 当开证行拒绝付款或保兑行拒绝付款和议付，并已经按照本条款要求发出通知时，该银行将有权就已经履行的偿付索取退款及其利息。

［讲解］

本条涉及关于单据与信用证不符而遭到银行拒付的问题。信用证的性质决定了银行（包括最后的开证行）支付款项的依据，必须是单、证相符。如果单、证不符，银行可以拒付。例如，D银行对要求办理出口押汇的 A 出口公司履行了议付的手续，购买了 A 公司递交单、证相符的单据，将货款扣除利息和相关费用后，余数付给 A 公司。

现在的问题是：A 公司拿到押汇得来的款项可不可以使用？按常理分析，这笔款当然可以自由使用。但现在情况却不是这样，作为国内的议付银行，强调议付的款项可以追索，也就是说：当 D 银行由于单、证等原因从开证行处拿不到款项时，它便可以向 A 公司追回已付出的款项（还包括利息），这就是“追索”。这样，办理了押汇的 A 出口公司处于两难的地位。如将押汇得来的款使用了，一旦发生“追索”怎么办？如不使用款项，那办理押汇有什么意义？笔者认为：产生这个问题最主要原因在于议付行的业务能力不过硬，一旦遇到开证行拒付时，不能（或基本不能）理直气壮地就开证行指出的所谓不符点与之交涉，而只是向出口方追回已付出的款项而已。根据本条及相关条规定的精神，议付行完全可以做到议付后不再追索，也就是不保留追索权（without recourse），这点并非不能做到。据了解，有些在我国开业的外资银行已经有了这样的承诺。如果我们出口地银行加强业务培训，掌握国际惯例，提高审单能力，一旦遇到国外拒付时，能够据理力争，不难做到银行向客户承诺不保留议付追索权这个多年解决不了的问题。如果真能做到这点，将会大大促进出口贸易。

1. 本条详细规定开证行对单证不符的单据的处置办法，包括：拒付、征求开证人是否接受有问题的单据，或保持有问题的单证，等待交单方进一步指示等。

2. 本条明确规定，当提交的单据出现单证不符时。开证行/保兑行/被指定银行应该一次性地就单证中的不符点向单证的提交人发出通知并表明银行的处理意见，包括如下。

(1) 拒付款项。

(2) 指出单证内银行据以拒付的不符点，及对有问题单证的处理措施如下。

a. 银行暂时保存单据，等待单据提交方进一步指示。

b. 银行暂时保存单据，直到申请人表态接受该套有问题的单据。同时，银行也表示同意申请人的这个要求。

c. 在申请人表态前，银行已从单据提交方得到进一步指示，并已按指示去处理有问题的单证。

(3) 银行将单证退回原处。

(4) 照先前单据提交人的指示处理单据。

3. 当银行拒绝付款的理由确凿，并发出单证不符的通知后，它就有权索回已经偿付的款项和利息。

[与第500号出版物比较]

本条是照第500号出版物的第十四条内容的精神制定的，但措辞语气更肯定、明确。处理单证的日期也明确地从7天改为5天。

[原文] Article 17 Original Documents and Copies

a. At least one original of each document stipulated in the credit must be presented.

b. A bank shall treat as an original any document bearing an apparently original signature, mark, stamp, or label of the issuer of the document, unless the document itself indicates that it is not an original.

c. Unless a document indicates otherwise, a bank will also accept a document as original if it:

i. appears to be written, typed, perforated or stamped by the document issuer's hand; or

ii. appears to be on the document issuer's original stationery; or

iii. states that it is original, unless the statement appears not to apply to the document presented.

d. If a credit requires presentation of copies of documents, presentation of either originals or copies is permitted.

e. If a credit requires presentation of multiple documents by using terms such as "in duplicate", "in two fold" or "in two copies", this will be satisfied by the presentation of at least one original and the remaining number in copies, except when the document itself indicates otherwise.

[译文] 第十七条 正本单据和副本单据

a. 信用证中规定的每种单据必须提交至少一份正本。

b. 除非单据本身表明其不是正本，银行将视任何表面上具有单据出具人正本签字、标志、图章或标签的单据为正本单据。

c. 除非单据另有陈述，如果单据符合以下条件，银行将接受该单据作为正本单据：

i. 表面上显示由单据出具人手写、打字、穿孔签字或盖章；或

ii. 表面上显示使用的是单据出具人的正本信笺；或

iii. 声明单据为正本，除非该项声明表面显示出与所提示的单据不符。

d. 如果信用证要求提交副本单据，则提交正本单据或副本单据均可。

e. 如果信用证中使用诸如“一式两份”、“两张”、“两份”等术语要求提交多份单据，则可以通过提交至少一份正本，其余为副本来满足信用证要求。但单据本身另有其他指示的除外。

[讲解]

1. 本条对“正本”单据的含义，作了明确的规定。文内指出：除非单据本身表明或显示不是正本。凡是符合下列情况之一者，都可算为正本单据。

(1) 单据表面具有单据出具人 a. 正本签字 b. 标志 c. 图章 d. 标签。

(2) 单据表面由单据出具人 a. 手工书写 b. 打字 c. 穿孔签字 d. 盖章。

(3) 单据出具人的正本信笺。

(4) 声明单据是正本。

2. 本条对正本单据的份数也有规定，指出：凡信用证内规定要提供多份单据，诸如“一式两份”、“两张”、“两份”等，在处理时至少要提供一份正本，其余用副本来满足云云。笔者认为，在实际业务中，如果来证规定要提供“一式两份”、“两张”、“两份”单据时，应提供两张正本为宜。因为多数银行向外寄出单据时，为防止单据丢失，习惯做法是分两批（two lots）寄出，如果仅有一份正本，其余是副本，一旦正本单据丢失，就会影响提取货物（如正本提单丢失，则不能提货）或保险索赔（如正本保险单丢失，则不能办理索赔），使当事人的利益受到损失。

[与第 500 号出版物比较]

1. 第 500 号出版物内，只是在第二十条对单据的正、副本做了一些规定，不似第 600 号出版物对单据的正、副本单独列出一条。由此可以看出国际上业内人士对正本单据的重视，也体现银行与交单方长期对“正本”的含义和份数的理解不一致，有必要统一对这方面的认识。

2. 本条删除旧惯例对于用影印和复写方式制作的单据认可为正本的规定。但增加可以视作正本单据的条件。如：“标志”(mark)、“标签”（label)、“表面看来使用单据出具人的正本信笺”（appears to be on the document issuer's original stationary）以及“声明该单据为正本，除非该项声明看来与所提示的单据不符”（states that it is original, unless the statement appears not to apply to the document presented）等。这样就对“正本”的含义更加明确，更便于掌握。

[原文] **Article 18 Commercial Invoice**

a. A commercial invoice:

i. must appear to have been issued by the beneficiary (except as provided in article 38);

ii. must be made out in the name of the applicant (except as provided in sub-article 38 (g));

iii. must be made out in the same currency as the credit; and

iv. need not be signed.

b. A nominated bank acting on its nomination, a confirming bank, if any, orthe issuing bank may accept a commercial invoice issued for an amount in excess of the amount permitted by the credit, and its decision will be binding upon all parties, provided the bank in question has not honoured or negotiated for an amount in excess of that permitted by the credit.

c. The description of the goods, services or performance in a commercial invoice must correspond with that appearing in the credit.

[译文] 第十八条 商业发票

a. 商业发票：

i. 必须表面看来系由受益人出具（第三十八条另有规定的除外）；

ii. 必须做成申请人抬头（第三十八条（g）款另有规定的除外）；

iii. 必须做成与信用证中规定的币种相同；

iv. 无须签字。

b. 按照指定行事的指定银行、保兑行（如有）或开证行可以接受超过信用证所允许金额出具的商业发票。如果有关银行已经付款或议付的金额未超过信用证所允许的金额，则该银行的决定对有关各方均具有约束力。

c. 商业发票中货物、服务或行为的描述必须与信用证规定的内容一致。

[讲解]

在每份信用证内规定受益人提供的众多单据中，商业发票是绝不可少的。它也是在众多单据中内容最多、最完善的单据。如有的单证内没有显示商品的唛头（如汇票），没有显示商品的单价及金额（如提单）等，商业发票都具备以上内容。同时，商业发票的用途比较广泛，除供结算款项使用外，在进、出口报关、买卖双方计账、核对货物等方面，商业发票往往都作为主要参考和依据，由此可见商业发票的重要性。

1. 别的单据的出具人可以不是信用证上的受益人，但商业发票必须由受益人出具。

2. 发票上的抬头人（即接受发票者、付款人），必须是信用证上的开证人。

3. 本条规定：发票不用签字。但笔者认为：发票上应该印有出具人的名称，但有的发票却不是这样，除了印有“发票”两字外，基本上是白纸一张，如不加盖有出具人名称的印章，则根本不知是哪家公司出具的发票。因此，遇有上述情况时，应在发票上标明出具人的单位名称或盖上出具人单位图章，以利于辨认。

4. 发票的底端通常印有 E. & O. E（errors & omissions excepted）即“有错当查”，指发票内出现差错时，允许制单人更正。但有时开证人要求受益人提供的不是一般商业发票，而是“证实发票”（certified invoice）。则在制作发票时，先将“有错当查”字删去，制作发票要更加仔细，因为将“有错当查”划去后，意味发票内容一旦有错，是不允许更改的。

[与第 500 号出版物比较]

本条沿用第 500 号出版物的第三十七条内部分内容。没有太大更动的地方。

[原文] Article 19　Transport Document Covering at Least Two Different Modes of Transport

a. A transport document covering at least two different modes of transport (multimodal or combined transport document), however named, must appear to:

i. indicate the name of the carrier and be signed by:

- the carrier or a named agent for or on behalf of the carrier, or
- the master or a named agent for or on behalf of the master.

Any signature by the carrier, master or agent must be identified as that of the carrier, master or agent.

Any signature by an agent must indicate whether the agent has signed for or on behalf of the carrier or for or on behalf of the master.

ii. indicate that the goods have been dispatched, taken in charge or shipped on board at the place stated in the credit, by:

• pre-printed wording, or

• a stamp or notation indicating the date on which the goods have been dispatched, taken in charge or shipped on board.

The date of issuance of the transport document will be deemed to be the date of dispatch, taking in charge or shipped on board, and the date of shipment. However, if the transport document indicates, by stamp or notation, a date of dispatch, taking in charge or shipped on board, this date will be deemed to be the date of shipment.

iii. indicate the place of dispatch, taking in charge or shipment and the place of final destination stated in the credit, even if:

a) the transport document states, in addition, a different place of dispatch, taking in charge or shipment or place of final destination, or

b) the transport document contains the indication "intended" or similar qualification in relation to the vessel, port of loading or port of discharge.

iv. be the sole original transport document or, if issued in more than one original, be the full set as indicated on the transport document.

v. contain terms and conditions of carriage or make reference to another source containing the terms and conditions of carriage (short form or blank back transport document). Contents of terms and conditions of carriage will not be examined.

vi. contain no indication that it is subject to a charter party.

b. For the purpose of this article, transhipment means unloading from one means of conveyance and reloading to another means of conveyance (whether or not in different modes of transport) during the carriage from the place of dispatch, taking in charge or shipment to the place of final destination stated in the credit.

c. i. A transport document may indicate that the goods will or may be transhipped provided that the entire carriage is covered by one and the same transport document.

ii. A transport document indicating that transhipment will or may take place is acceptable, even if the credit prohibits transhipment.

[译文] 第十九条 至少包括两种不同运输方式的运输单据

a. 至少包括两种不同运输方式的运输单据（即多式运输单据或联合运输单据），不论其称谓如何，必须表面看来：

i. 注明承运人名称并由下列人员签署：

- 承运人或作为承运人的具名代理或代表，或
- 船长或作为船长的具名代理或代表。

代理的签字必须注明其是作为承运人的代理或代表还是船长的代理或代表签字的。

ii. 通过下述方式表明货物已在信用证规定的地点发运、接受监管或装船：

- 预先印就的词语，或
- 有显示货物已发运、接受监管或装船的日期的图章或批注。

运输单据的出具日期将被认为是货物发运、接受监管或已装船及装运的日期。

然而，如果运输单据以盖章或批注方式注明发运、接受监管或装船的日期，则此日期将被视为装运日期。

iii. 注明信用证中规定的发运、接受监管或装运地点及最终目的地的地点，即使：

a）运输单据另外表明了不同的发运、接受监管、装船或最终目的地的地点，或

b）运输单据含有“预期”或类似有关限定船只、装货港或卸货港的要求。

iv. 可以是仅有的一份正本运输单据，或者，如果出具了一份以上正本运输单据，则应该是运输单据中标明的全套正本份数。

v. 含有的承运条款须参阅包含承运条款的某一出处（简式或背面空白的运输单据），银行对此类承运条款的内容不予审核。

vi. 未注明运输单据受租船合约约束。

b. 就本条款而言，转运意指信用证中规定的货物从发运、接受监管、装船到最终目的地的运输过程中，从某个运输工具卸下再重新装上另一个运输工具上（无论是否为不同运输方式）的运输方式。

c. i. 只要同一运输单据包括运输全程，则运输单据可以注明货物即将或可能被转运。

ii. 即使信用证禁止转运，银行也将接受注明转运即将或可能发生的运输单据。

[讲解]

1. 本条的标题是“至少包括两种不同运输方式的单据”，指出运输方式至少在两种或两种以上。这种写法，比一般书上直接称作“多式联运单据”更为确切。在“至少包括不同运输方式”中，运输方式可以包括海运（水运），也可以不包括海运（水运）。

2. 对于货物装运后，货运单据签发人的资格问题，过去基本没有涉及，往往在目的地提货时由于运输单据签发人的资格而发生纠纷，影响正常提货程序，甚至发生运输单据签发人欺诈行为。本条对运输单据的签发人的身份有具体规定，要求运输单据的签发人：有明确身份的承运人，或承运人明确身份的代理人。或明确身份船长，或船长明确身份的代理人所签发的运输提单

(指两种以上运输方式包括一程是海运/水运，所以要有提单)。之所以对海运提单的签发提出具体要求。笔者认为：因为海上运输仍是当前国际贸易最主要的运输方式，而且海运提单在制作上较其他运输单据复杂。

3. 本条对至少包括两种不同运输方式单据/提单的签发，要求符合以下要求。

第一种　明确身份的承运人所签发的提单——由明确承运人身份的负责人 Henry 先生签发至少包括两种不同运输方式单据/提单。如：

ABC Shipping Co. Ltd.

Henry——负责人签字

As carrier (As carrier)

第二种　明确身份的代理人代承运人签发的至少包括两种不同运输方式单据 / 提单——由承运人 ABC 海运公司的代理人 TSS 公司负责人 Johnson 先生签发联运单据 / 联运提单。如：

TSS Co., Ltd.

Johnson——负责人签字

As agent for (or as agent on behalf of)

ABC Shipping Co., Ltd.

The carrier

第三种　明确身份的船长签发的提单——由承运人 ABC 海运公司船长 Jack 先生签发的至少包括两种运输方式提单（包括海运/水运）。如：

Jack（船长签字）

Master of

ABC Shipping Co., Ltd.

The carrier

第四种　明确身份的代理人代船长签发的至少包括两种不同运输方式提单（包括海运/水运）——由承运人 ABC 海运公司的

船长 Jack 先生的代理人 Smith 公司的 Ken 先生签发联运单据/联运提单。如：

Smith Co.（代理人公司）

Ken（签字）

As agent for (or as agent on behalf of)

Jackson

Master of ABC Shipping Co., Ltd.

The carrier

4. 本条内对货物"装运"包含货物在规定的地点发运、接受监管或装载。这实际上将贸易术语与"装运"结合起来。因为当前用得最多的贸易术语是国际商会制定的《2000年国际贸易术语解释通则》（INCOTERMS 2000）。其中对 FOB、CFR、CIF 等术语的解释是：卖方的风险必须待货物越过船舷后才告结束。运输起讫是从装运港至目的港，两头都是港口。而对 FCA、CPT、CIP 等术语的释是：卖方的风险是将货物交付承运人后就告结束。运输的起讫是装运地（港）至目的地（港）。两组术语所标明买/卖方的风险划分，显然有明显区别，如果多式运输就不应使用 FOB、CFR 和 CIF 术语，因为这组术语只适合单一的海（水）运方式。所以，本条规定明确结合贸易术语解释，便于理解、操作。

5. 由于至少有两种不同的运输方式，因此，在运输单据方面与单纯一种运输方式的单据不同。本条根据实际情况，规定有4个与货物交接有关的地点。即接受监管地（place of receipt），它可与装货港（port of loading）/地不同。货物最后到达的目的地（place of delivery），它可与卸货港（port of discharge）/卸货地（place of discharge）不一样。

例如，有一批货物采用多式运输方式从西安运到维也纳。在运输单据应这样填写：

Place of receipt : Xi'an（西安）

Port of loading: Xingang of Tianjin（天津新港）

Port of discharge: Hamburg（汉堡）

Place of delivery: Vienna（维也纳）

在具体业务中，也有从西安到汉堡，或在天津新港用船将货运到汉堡。这时的收货地就与目的地一致，都是汉堡。如果将货物从天津新港装船运到维也纳，则监管地就和装运港一致，都在天津新港。收货人一般最关心的是在信用证内规定在何地交货（当使用 FCA、EXW 贸易术语时）和在何地收货（当使用 CPT、CIP 以及 DDU、DDP 等贸易术语），只要在这方面满足证内要求，收货人及银行就不会介意船只、装货及卸货港口有“预期/定”字样。因为即使船只、装货及卸货港口有变化，不会影响承运人把货物运到信用证内规定的目的地。

6. 对运输单据的正本份数，本条也做了明确规定：一份正本或多份正本，但多份正本的份数，必须要和运输单据上所显示的数字一致。如规定运输单据要“正本签字提单 3 份”（signed 3 original B/L），则受益人交付给银行的正本提单也应该是 3 份。这样做可以避免某些开证人要求受益人将其中一份正本提单（或多式运输单据），不通过银行而直接寄给开证人，因此对受益人产生的风险。

7. 由于涉及的是两种或以上不同的运输方式，所以必然会有“转运”这个环节（即从这种运输方式转换为另一种运输方式），否则就不能称为“至少包括两种以上不同的运输方式”。所以，在信用证内，应该对“转运”有相应的规定。本条规定：“即使信用证禁止转运（这本来就不合理），银行也将接受注明转运将发生或可能发生的运输单据”。这样的规定，无疑是很合理的。

[与第 500 号出版物比较]

1. 本条内一些规定，基本上和第 500 号出版物中的第二十条、二十六条类似，但将某些提法做了更改和删除。如删除“……仅以风帆为动力”。现在国际贸易的运输工具，已经没有以风帆为动力的运输工具。再有类似规定，显然没有意义。

2. 第500号出版物的第二十六条规定“多式运输单据”的签发人有承运人或多式运输营运人（multimodal transport operator）以及他的具名代理或代表等。第600号出版物删去“多式运输营运人”，笔者认为：这样做有一定的含义，因为“多式运输营运人”一般也就指的是货运代理——“货代”。目前，在众多“货代”中，它们的规模、资信、经营能力等方面各不相同，差距甚大，如果不考虑它们的具体情况，笼统地将签发“多式运输单据”的权限交给它们，显然不够妥当，甚至出现过一些资信不良的“货代”与当事人相互勾结，给对方造成极坏影响或经济损失的现象。所以，本条将“多式运输营运人”签发运输单据的内容删除，是有道理的。

3. 由于是多种运输方式运输，所以本条用“已装运”（shipped on board）代替第500号出版物的“已装船”（loaded on board）。意即货物不一定是装船，也可以装上其他运输工具，如火车、飞机等，这样就更加显示“多式运输”中的“多式”特点。

［原文］Article 20　Bill of Lading

a. A bill of lading, however named, must appear to:

i. indicate the name of the carrier and be signed by:

- the carrier or a named agent for or on behalf of the carrier, or
- the master or a named agent for or on behalf of the master.

Any signature by the carrier, master or agent must be identified as that of the carrier, master or agent.

Any signature by an agent must indicate whether the agent has signed for or on behalf of the carrier or for or on behalf of the master.

ii. indicate that the goods have been shipped on board a named vessel at the port of loading stated in the credit by:

- pre-printed wording, or
- an on board notation indicating the date on which the goods have been shipped on board.

The date of issuance of the bill of lading will be deemed to be the date of shipment unless the bill of lading contains an on board notation indicating the date of shipment, in which case the date stated in the on board notation will be deemed to be the date of shipment.

If the bill of lading contains the indication "intended vessel" or similar qualification in relation to the name of the vessel, an on board notation indicating the date of shipment and the name of the actual vessel is required.

iii. indicate shipment from the port of loading to the port of discharge stated in the credit.

If the bill of lading does not indicate the port of loading stated in the credit as the port of loading, or if it contains the indication "intended" or similar qualification in relation to the port of loading, an on board notation indicating the port of loading as stated in the credit, the date of shipment and the name of the vessel is required. This provision applies even when loading on board or shipment on a named vessel is indicated by pre-printed wording on the bill of lading.

iv. be the sole original bill of lading or, if issued in more than one original, be the full set as indicated on the bill of lading.

v. contain terms and conditions of carriage or make reference to another source containing the terms and conditions of carriage (short form or blank back bill of lading). Contents of terms and conditions of carriage will not be examined.

vi. contain no indication that it is subject to a charter party.

b. For the purpose of this article, transhipment means unloading from one vessel and reloading to another vessel during the carriage from the port of loading to the port of discharge stated in the credit.

c. i. A bill of lading may indicate that the goods will or may be transhipped provided that the entire carriage is covered by one and the same bill of lading.

ii. A bill of lading indicating that transhipment will or may take place is acceptable, even if the credit prohibits transhipment, if the goods have been shipped in a container, trailer or LASH barge as evidenced by the bill of lading.

d. Clauses in a bill of lading stating that the carrier reserves the right to tranship will be disregarded.

[译文] 第二十条　提单

a. 不论其称谓如何，提单必须表面上看来：

i. 注明承运人名称并由下列人员签署：

承运人或作为承运人的具名代理或代表，或

船长或作为船长的具名代理或代表。

承运人、船长或代理的任何签字必须分别表明承运人、船长或代理的身份。

代理的签字必须表明其是作为承运人还是作为船长的代理或代表签署提单。

ii. 通过下述方式表明货物已在信用证规定的装运港装上具名船只：

预先印就的词语，或

注明货物装船日期的装船批注。

提单的出具日期将被视为装运日期，除非提单包含表明装运日期的已装船批注，此时装船批注中注明的日期将被视为装运日期。

如果提单包含“预期船”字样或类似有关限定船只的词语时，装船批注必须注明装运日期以及实际装运的船名。

iii. 注明承运从信用证中规定的装货港至卸货港。

如果提单未注明信用证中规定的装货港为装货港，或者包含“预期”或类似有关限定装货港的词语，则装船批注中必须注明信用证规定的装货港、装运日期以及船名。即使提单上标明预先印就的“已装船”或“已装具名船只”词语，本规定仍然适用。

iv. 可以是仅有的一份正本提单，或者，如果出具了一份以上正本提单，则应是提单中标明的全套正本份数。

v. 含有的承运条款须参阅包含承运条款的某一出处（简式或背面空白的提单），银行对此类承运条款的内容不予审核。

vi. 未注明提单受租船合约约束。

b. 就本条款而言，转运意指从信用证中规定的装货港到卸货港的运输过程中，从某艘船卸下再重新装上另一艘船上的运输方式。

c. i. 只要同一提单包括运输全程，则提单可以注明货物即将或可能被转运。

ii. 银行可以接受注明将要发生或可能发生转运的提单。即使信用证禁止转运，只要提单证实有关货物已由集装箱、拖车或子母船运输，银行仍可接受注明即将或可能发生转运的提单。

d. 银行对于提单中声明承运人保留转运权利的条款将不予置理。

[讲解]

1. 本条对提单的签发者有具体要求，这种要求和至少包括两种以上不同运输方式单据的签发人基本一样。即：提单的签发人必须是承运人或承运人的具名代理或代表，或者船长或船长的具名代理或代表。并要求签发人在提单上表明他们的身份。为什么要有这样严格的规定？笔者认为，因为提单和至少包括两种不同运输方式单据的作用是一样的，都可以凭它提取货物，通过背书，还可以转让。所以，对这种运输单据要特别慎重。

2. 本条根据不同的贸易术语对提单有不同的要求。如FOB、CFR、CIF就必须签发“已装船提单”（on board B/L），但使用FCA、CPT、CIP术语用于海上运输时，承运人就可以签发“备运提单”（cargo received for shipment B/L）。因为两组贸易术语中关于风险的划分完全不同，前一组的卖方履行交货任务时，必须将货物越过船舷，才算“装船”（on board）。而后一组的卖方只要将货物交给承运人，承担的风险便告转移，将来再由承运人把货物装上已有船名的船上。这种做法，同样可以算作“装运”（shipment）。

3. 本条对于提单正本的规定很仔细。规定正本提单是一份或一份以上，如果开证人要求提供一份以上正本时，所提供正本提单的份数，应该和提单上所标明的数字一致。如来证要求提供三份正本提单时，受益人应按规定办理。提单上也要注明：“签发三份正本”。

4. 本条规定，即使信用证规定不允许转运，但只要提单上证实货物采用集装箱、子母船或拖车运输，银行可以接受将发生/可能发生转运的提单。因为集装箱必然有一段陆上运输。子母船也有从大船到小船或者小船到大船的转运过程。而拖车运输也是有一段距离不是海上运输。例如，货物装上拖车后，从生产厂/仓库运上船或连车带货都留在船上。当船抵达目的港口后，拖车从船上开出，将货物运到收货人处。因此，信用证规定“不允许转运”显然是不妥当的。

[与第500号出版物比较]

本条与第500号出版物中第二十三条中的一些规定相近，但本条的内容，有的地方更加简化，便于掌握。

1. 由于用在海运的贸易术语所包含的风险划分不同，有的术语规定货物必须越过船舷，有的则规定货物交给承运人。所以，已装船提单的签发日期就可以作为货物已经装完船的日期。而备运提单的签发日期也可以当作装船日期，如果信用证内没有特别要求，就没有必要在备运提单上批注实际的装船日期。

2. 本条中虽有一些规定与旧惯例相似。但即使在相似的地方，也删除或用其他更加明确的词句，取代原有的一些不肯定、不明确的词句。诸如“除非信用证条款禁止转运”、“除非信用证另有规定”、“以其他方式证实”及“视情况而定”等。

［原文］Article 21　Non-Negotiable Sea Waybill

a. A non-negotiable sea waybill, however named, must appear to:

i. indicate the name of the carrier and be signed by:

- the carrier or a named agent for or on behalf of the carrier, or
- the master or a named agent for or on behalf of the master.

Any signature by the carrier, master or agent must be identified as that of the carrier, master or agent.

Any signature by an agent must indicate whether the agent has signed for or on behalf of the carrier or for or on behalf of the master.

ii. indicate that the goods have been shipped on board a named vessel at the port of loading stated in the credit by:

- pre-printed wording, or
- an on board notation indicating the date on which the goods have been shipped on board.

The date of issuance of the non-negotiable sea waybill will be deemed to be the date of shipment unless the non-negotiable sea waybill contains an on board notation indicating the date of shipment, in which case the date stated in the on board notation will be deemed to be the date of shipment.

If the non-negotiable sea waybill contains the indication “intended vessel" or similar qualification in relation to the name of the vessel, an on board notation indicating the date of shipment and the name of the actual vessel is required.

iii. indicate shipment from the port of loading to the port of discharge stated in the credit.

If the non-negotiable sea waybill does not indicate the port of loading stated in the credit as the port of loading, or if it contains the indication "intended" or similar qualification in relation to the port of loading, an on board notation indicating the port of loading as stated in the credit, the date of shipment and the name of the vessel is required. This provision applies even when loading on board or shipment on a named vessel is indicated by pre-printed wording on the non-negotiable sea waybill.

iv. be the sole original non-negotiable sea waybill or, if issued in more than one original, be the full set as indicated on the non-negotiable sea waybill.

v. contain terms and conditions of carriage or make reference to another source containing the terms and conditions of carriage (short form or blank back non-negotiable sea waybill). Contents of terms and conditions of carriage will not be examined.

vi. contain no indication that it is subject to a charter party.

b. For the purpose of this article, transhipment means unloading from one vessel and reloading to another vessel during the carriage from the port of loading to the port of discharge stated in the credit.

c. i. A non-negotiable sea waybill may indicate that the goods will or may be transhipped provided that the entire carriage is covered by one and the same non-negotiable sea waybill.

ii. A non-negotiable sea waybill indicating that transhipment will or may take place is acceptable, even if the credit prohibits transhipment, if the goods have been shipped in a container, trailer or LASH barge as evidenced by the non-negotiable sea waybill.

d. Clauses in a non-negotiable sea waybill stating that the carrier reserves the right to tranship will be disregarded.

[译文] 第二十一条　非转让海运单

a. 不论其称谓如何，非转让海运单必须表面上看来：

i. 注明承运人名称并由下列人员签署：

承运人或作为承运人的具名代理或代表，或

船长或作为船长的具名代理或代表。

承运人、船长或代理的任何签字必须分别表明承运人、船长或代理的身份。

代理的签字必须表明其是作为承运人还是船长的代理或代表签署提单。

ii. 通过下述方式表明货物已在信用证规定的装运港装上具名船只：

预先印就的词语，或

注明货物装船日期的装船批注。

非转让海运单的出具日期将被视为装运日期，除非非转让海运单包含表明装运日期的已装船批注，此时装船批注中注明的日期将被视为装运日期。

如果非转让海运单包含“预期船”字样或类似有关限定船只的词语时，装船批注必须注明装运日期以及实际装运的船名。

iii. 注明承运从信用证中规定的装货港至卸货港。

如果非转让海运单未注明信用证中规定的装货港为装货港，或者包含“预期”或类似有关限定装货港的词语，则装船批注必须注明信用证规定的装货港、装运日期以及船名。即使非转让海运单上标明预先印就的“已装船”或“已装具名船只”词语，本规定仍然适用。

iv. 可以是仅有的一份正本非转让海运单，或者，如果出具了一份以上正本非转让海运单，应是非转让海运单中标明的全套正本份数。

v. 含有的承运条款须参阅包含承运条款的某一出处（简式或背面空白的非转让海运单），银行对此类承运条款的内容不予审核。

vi. 未注明非转让海运单受租船合约约束。

b. 就本条款而言，转运意指在信用证规定的装货港到卸货港之间的海运过程中，将货物由一艘船卸下再装上另一艘船的运输方式。

c. i. 只要同一非转让海运单包括运输全程，则非转让海运单可以注明货物即将或可能被转运。

ii. 银行可以接受注明将要发生或可能发生转运的非转让海运单。即使信用证禁止转运，只要非转让海运单上证实有关货物已由集装箱、拖车或子母船运输，银行仍可接受注明即将或可能发生转运的非转让海运单。

d. 银行对于非转让海运单中声明承运人保留转运权利的条款将不予置理。

[讲解]

1. 非转让海运单的使用，远在海运提单之后。由于它不能提货、不能流通，因而限定了它的使用范围。一般认为：随着国际贸易向EDI（电子数据交换）发展，使用非转让海运单的领域，将会日益扩大。笔者认为：这种运输单据的使用，主要是为收货人服务的。由于收货人不打算再转让货物，同时也担心单据在寄送过程中发生丢失，所以要求托运人提供这种形式的运输单据。

2. 非转让海运单在单据的性质、作用方面，与海运提单中的“空白提单”（open B/L）和“指示提单”（order B/L）完全不同，后两种提单可以提货、通过背书手续（空白提单可以不背书）后，还可以流通。但非转让海运单和海运提单中的“记名提单”（straight B/L），却有类似的地方，两者的收货人是固定的，都不能流通。记名提单中的记名收货人可以凭提单提货，而非转让海运单不能提货，当海运公司将货物运抵目的港后，便向运单上的收货人发出“到货通知”。收货人须凭通知和证明身份的证件，办理提货手续。虽然非转让海运单和海运提单的反差极大，但两者都是海洋运输单据，在有关运输的栏目、细节和做法上是基本一致的。如两种单据都有以下栏目：托运人、收货人、通知人、船名、航次、启运港、卸货港、唛头、货名、件数、毛重体积及运费支付等项。因此，本条对非转让海运单的规定，与上条对海运提单的规定基本上是一致的。

3. 非转让海运单在许多方面和“空运运单”（air way waybill）以及“国际铁路联运运单”（international railway through-transport bill）有相似处。例如，收货人是固定的，都不能凭以提货。收货人提货时都是凭运输公司、航空公司和铁路局发出的“到货通知”和本人的有效证件，办理提货手续。都不能流通。由于这三种运输单据都有相同的特点，因此，托运人（卖方）在制作单据时要特别仔细。因为托运人将货物发运后，实际上已经丧失了对货物的控制权。在使用信用证的情况下，如果缮制的单据内容有错误，造成单证不符，就会失去银行信用的保障，进而导致货款落空的损失。

[与第 500 号出版物相比较]

本条与第 500 号出版物中的第二十四条内容相似。但本条删除原规定的一些内容，如删除“除非信用证另有规定”、“或者以其他方式证实”及“视情况而定”等，与上条所删改的内容一样。本条经整理后，内容更为严谨、具体。

［原文］Article 22　Charter Party Bill of Lading

a. A bill of lading, however named, containing an indication that it is subject to a charter party (charter party bill of lading), must appear to:

i. be signed by:

- the master or a named agent for or on behalf of the master, or
- the owner or a named agent for or on behalf of the owner, or
- the charterer or a named agent for or on behalf of the charterer.

Any signature by the master, owner, charterer or agent must be identified as that of the master, owner, charterer or agent.

Any signature by an agent must indicate whether the agent has signed for or on behalf of the master, owner or charterer.

An agent signing for or on behalf of the owner or charterer must indicate the name of the owner or charterer.

ii. indicate that the goods have been shipped on board a named vessel at the port of loading stated in the credit by:

- pre-printed wording, or
- an on board notation indicating the date on which the goods have been shipped on board.

The date of issuance of the charter party bill of lading will be deemed to be the date of shipment unless the charter party bill of lading contains an on board notation indicating the date of shipment, in which case the date stated in the on board notation will be deemed to be the date of shipment.

iii. indicate shipment from the port of loading to the port of discharge stated in the credit. The port of discharge may also be shown as a range of ports or a geographical area, as stated in the credit.

iv. be the sole original charter party bill of lading or, if issued in more than one original, be the full set as indicated on the charter party bill of lading.

b. A bank will not examine charter party contracts, even if they are required to be presented by the terms of the credit.

[译文] 第二十二条　租船合约提单

a. 不论称谓如何，只要提单中包括受租船合约约束的指示(即租船合约提单)，则必须在表面看来：

i. 由下列人员签署：

船长或作为船长的具名代理或代表，或者

船东或作为船东的具名代理或代表，或者

租船人或作为租船人的具名代理或代表。

船长、船东、租船人或代理的任何签字必须分别表明其船长、船东、租船人或代理的身份。

代理的签字必须表明是作为船长还是作为船东或是作为租船人的代理或代表签署提单。

代理人代理或代表船东或租船人签署提单时必须注明船东或租船人的名称。

ii. 通过下述方式表明货物已在信用证规定的装运港装上具名船只：

预先印就的词语，或

注明货物装船日期的装船批注。

租船合约提单的出具日期将被视为装运日期，除非租船合约提单包含表明装运日期的已装船批注，此时装船批注中注明的日期将被视为装运日期。

iii. 注明承运从信用证中规定的装货港至卸货港。卸货港可以标明为信用证的规定港口范围或地理区域。

iv. 可以是仅有的一份正本租船合约提单，或者，如果出具了一份以上正本租船合约提单，应是租船合约提单中标明的全套正本份数。

b. 即使根据信用证的条款要求提交租船合约，银行也将不予审核该租船合约。

[讲解]

1. 本条要求签发提单人与一般海洋提单的签发者有相同处，也有不同处：a. 船长或船长的具名代理或代表——相同。b. 船东或船东的具名代理或代表——不同。c. 租船人或租船人的具名代理或代表——不同。

2. 本条没有规定银行对租船合约提单的态度。因此，当受益人提交租船合约提单时，银行不会加以干涉。当信用证规定要求受益人交付的单据中包括租船合约时，银行自然也不审核该合约的内容。

3. 本条对其他部分的规定，如：提单份数、装运日、装运港与卸货港等与对海运提单的要求基本一致。

[与第500号出版物比较]

本条与第500号出版物的第二十五条中有的内容相似，但有明显不同处，表现如下。

1. 原第二十五条规定除非信用证规定可接受租船合约提单，否则银行拒收该种提单。但在本条款中，删除了这项规定，这不仅说明银行对这项内容在管理上放宽，也说明租船合约提单在应用上将日渐增多。

2. 增加“租船人或租船人的具名代理或代表”有权签发提单的规定。

[原文] **Article 23　Air Transport Document**

a. An air transport document, however named, must appear to:

i. indicate the name of the carrier and be signed by:

- the carrier, or
- a named agent for or on behalf of the carrier.

Any signature by the carrier or agent must be identified as that of the carrier or agent.

Any signature by an agent must indicate that the agent has signed for or on behalf of the carrier.

ii. indicate that the goods have been accepted for carriage.

iii. indicate the date of issuance. This date will be deemed to be the date of shipment unless the air transport document contains a specific notation of the actual date of shipment, in which case the date stated in the notation will be deemed to be the date of shipment.

Any other information appearing on the air transport document relative to the flight number and date will not be considered in determining the date of shipment.

iv. indicate the airport of departure and the airport of destination stated in the credit.

v. be the original for consignor or shipper, even if the credit stipulates a full set of originals.

vi. contain terms and conditions of carriage or make reference to another source containing the terms and conditions of carriage. Contents of terms and conditions of carriage will not be examined.

b. For the purpose of this article, transhipment means unloading from one aircraft and reloading to another aircraft during the carriage from the airport of departure to the airport of destination stated in the credit.

c. i. An air transport document may indicate that the goods will or may be transhipped, provided that the entire carriage is covered by one and the same air transport document.

ii. An air transport document indicating that transhipment will or may take place is acceptable, even if the credit prohibits transhipment.

[译文] 第二十三条　空运单据

a. 不论称谓如何，空运单据必须在表面看来：

i. 注明承运人名称并由下列人员签署：

承运人，或

作为承运人的具名代理或代表。

承运人或代理的任何签字必须分别表明其承运人或代理的身份。代理的签字必须表明其作为承运人的代理或代表签署空运单据。

ii. 注明货物已收妥待运。

iii. 注明出具日期。该出具日期将被视为装运日期，除非空运单据包含表明实际装运日期的特别批注，此时批注中注明的日期将被视为装运日期。空运单据上表明的有关航班号和起飞日期任何信息不能被视为装运日期。

iv. 注明信用证规定的发运机场及目的地机场。

v. 只要是开给委托人或发货人的正本空运单据之一即可，即使信用证规定提交全套正本。

vi. 包含的承运条款，或者提示条款参见某一出处，银行将对此类承运条款的内容不予审核。

b. 就本条款而言，转运意指在信用证规定的起飞机场到目的地机场的运输过程中，将货物从一架飞机上卸下再装上另一架飞机的运输方式。

c. i. 只要同一空运单据包含运输全程，空运单据可以注明货物即将或可能被转运。

ii. 即使信用证禁止转运，银行仍可接受注明即将或可能发生转运的空运单据。

[讲解]

1. 空运单据——一般指“航空运单”（air waybill——AWB）。

它的性质和作用，与国际铁路联运运单相同，都是不代表货物所有权，不能提货，也不能转让流通。由于货物运到目的地后，航空公司在当地的代理直接通知收货人。后者凭“到货通知”和有关身份证明提货。由于来证经常规定航空运单上的收货人是开证人，因此，就要求受益人在制单时特别注意。因为一旦发生单证不符，受益人将丧失银行保障，而货早已被买主提走，将会造成经济上的损失。除非来证规定收货人是开证行，或者受益人要求对方将收货人更改，由原来规定的开证人改为开证行或受益人在当地的代理。

2. 本条规定，有资格签发空运运单的签发人是承运人或其代理。比允许签发海运提单的签发人要少。

3. 本条规定：航空运单显示的其他任何与航班号和起飞日期有关的信息，不能视为装运日期。这是因为：当托运人（货主）将货物交付承运人后，承运人就签发空运运单给托运人，这时飞机尚未起飞，实际起飞日期和航班号需要等货物运出后才能落实。所以，除信用证有特别规定，一般只将空运运单的出具日期，作为货物的装运日期对待。

4. 本条关于航空运单其他规定。如：银行是否审核承运条款、对转运的理解和处理等，基本和对海洋运输提单、非转让的海运单和租船合约提单相同。

[与第 500 号出版物比较]

本条与第 500 号出版物的第二十七条内容相似。个别处在用词上稍有更改。

[原文] Article 24　Road, Rail or Inland Waterway Transport Documents

a. A road, rail or inland waterway transport document, however named, must appear to:

i. indicate the name of the carrier and:

• be signed by the carrier or a named agent for or on behalf of the carrier, or

• indicate receipt of the goods by signature, stamp or notation by the carrier or a named agent for or on behalf of the carrier.

Any signature, stamp or notation of receipt of the goods by the carrier or agent must be identified as that of the carrier or agent.

Any signature, stamp or notation of receipt of the goods by the agent must indicate that the agent has signed or acted for or on behalf of the carrier.

If a rail transport document does not identify the carrier, any signature or stamp of the railway company will be accepted as evidence of the document being signed by the carrier.

ii. indicate the date of shipment or the date the goods have been received for shipment, dispatch or carriage at the place stated in the credit. Unless the transport document contains a dated reception stamp, an indication of the date of receipt or a date of shipment, the date of issuance of the transport document will be deemed to be the date of shipment.

iii. indicate the place of shipment and the place of destination stated in the credit.

b. i. A road transport document must appear to be the original for consignor or shipper or bear no marking indicating for whom the document has been prepared.

ii. A rail transport document marked "duplicate" will be accepted as an original.

iii. A rail or inland waterway transport document will be accepted as an original whether marked as an original or not.

c. In the absence of an indication on the transport document as to the number of originals issued, the number presented will be deemed to constitute a full set.

d. For the purpose of this article, transhipment means unloading from one means of conveyance and reloading to another means of conveyance, within the same mode of transport, during the carriage from the place of shipment, dispatch or carriage to the place of destination stated in the credit.

e. i. A road, rail or inland waterway transport document may indicate that the goods will or may be transhipped provided that the entire carriage is covered by one and the same transport document.

ii. A road, rail or inland waterway transport document indicating that transhipment will or may take place is acceptable, even if the credit prohibits transhipment.

［译文］第二十四条　公路、铁路或内河运输单据

a. 不论称谓如何，公路、铁路或内河运输单据，必须在表面看来：

i. 注明承运人名称，并且

由承运人或者作为承运人具名代理或代表签署，或者

由承运人或者作为承运人具名代理或代表以签字、印章或批注表明货物收讫。

承运人或代理表示货物收妥的签字、印章或批注必须分别表明承运人或代理人的身份。

代理的收妥签字、印戳或批注必须表明其作为承运人的代理或代表签字和行事。

如果铁路运输单据没有明确承运人，则银行可以接受以铁路运输公司的任何签字或印章来作为承运人签署单据的证明。

ii. 表明货物装运日期或者在信用证规定地点收妥待运、发运或承运的日期。除非运输单据上盖有带日期的货物收妥印章，或者注明了货物收讫日期、装运日期，运输单据的出具日期将被

视为装运日期。

iii. 表明信用证规定的发装运地和目的地。

b. i. 公路运输单据必须表面上看来是开给委托人或发运人，并且没有任何迹象表明出具人的正本单据已经备好。

ii. 注明“第二联”的铁路运输单据将被作为正本接受。

iii. 无论是否注明正本字样，铁路或内河运输单据都将被作为正本接受。

c. 如运输单据上未注明出具的正本份数，则提交的份数将被视为全套正本。

d. 就本条款而言，转运意指在信用证规定的装运、发运或承运的地点到目的地的运输过程中，用同一运输方式将货物从一个运输工具卸下再装上另一运输工具的运输方式。

e. i. 只要同一运输单据包含运输全程，公路、铁路或内河运输单据可以注明货物即将或可能被转运。

ii. 即使信用证禁止转运，银行仍可接受注明即将或可能发生转运的公路、铁路和内陆水运单据。

[讲解]

1. 本条强调，当采用不同的运输方式运送货物时，必须签发符合该种运输方式的单据。如经由公路运输的，要签发公路运输单据。如由铁路运输的，要签发铁路运输单据。关于铁路运输单据，有的书刊称之为“铁路运单”（railway bill）、“铁路托运单”（railway consignment note）等。笔者认为：本条所指的铁路运输是用于国际贸易的，与内地的做法不同，单据的形式和名称也就不同。目前，用于国际贸易的铁路单据，一种是“国际铁路联运运单”（International railway through-transport bill——此为英文译名，运单上使用中文和俄文）以及陆运输港（香港）使用的“承运货物收据”（cargo receipt）。两者含义、做法和作用有很大区别，不能混为一谈。至于在内陆使用水上运输的，则应签发内陆水运单据。

2. 本条规定公路、铁路和内陆水上运输单据的出具人，与上面几条的运输单据如海运提单、非流通海运单等运输方式单据的出具人，有相同处，也有不同处。如本条规定运输单据出具人可以是承运人，也可以是承运人具名的代理人。不同处是本条指出：如果铁路运输单据没有指明承运人，则（银行）可以接受铁路运输公司的任何人签字或印戳作为承运人签署单据的证据。笔者认为：这项规定非常适合内地的货物采用铁路运输方式运往香港的做法。现在的具体做法是：内地公司输往香港的货物装上火车后，由外贸运输公司（现称外贸运输集团）代表铁路方签发“承运货物收据”交托运人。为什么外运集团能够签发“收据”呢？因为外贸运输公司代表铁路方面，承接整个输往香港货物的运输、交接工作。如货物运到深圳后，还必须由当地外贸运输公司与港方办理货物的交接手续。货物经交接运到香港后，统一由香港中国旅行社以总收货人的身份将货收下，然后按“收据”上不同的收货人，分货物编号贮存。另一方面，当托运人办完发货环节所有手续后，将“承运货物收据”正本连同其他信用证内规定的单据，送交出口地银行结算货款。出口地银行将全套单据经审核无误后，寄至香港开证行，后者转而通知收货人付款赎单。收货人办完付款手续，便可持“承运货物收据”正本到香港中国旅行社联系提货。由此可见，“承运货物收据”与空运、公路运输单据不同，虽不能转让流通，但能代表货物所有权，是可以凭以提取货物的。

3. 关于铁路运输的另一种运输单据，“国际铁路联运运单”是由起运地铁路部门签发的，它的正本随车运行，副本交托运人。车辆至国境站后，由外贸运输公司与外方办理货物交接手续：包括换装车皮、清点货物 / 出具残损记录。货物运到目的地后，国外当地的铁路部门根据“国际铁路联运运单”上的名称和地址，通知收货人提货。后者在付清自卖方国境站交接以后所产生的一切费用（如运费、过境费、口岸报关费等）后，便可提取货物。

4. 填写“国际铁路联运运单”时，它的内容与一般运输单据不同，除收货人名称和地址外，还有“到达站”名和通过的国境站名。通过的国境站包括进、出国境站。如果站名一旦填写错误，将会造成货物运送不到或迂回运输的事故，所以要特别注意。

5. 本条其他方面的规定。如对单据正本的理解、正本单据份数、发运地/目的地及对货物转运的理解，与对海运、航空运输单据的规定相似。

［与第500号出版物比较］

本条内容与第500号出版物的第二十七条大体相似，为了更明确责任，有的词汇被删除掉，有的词汇被更改。如本条规定：只有三种日期才能被认为是发运日期——货物收妥待运/发运/承运日期（the date of the goods has been received for shipment/dispatch/carriage）。另外也增加“如果铁路运输单据没有指明承运人，可以接受铁路运输公司的任何签字或印戳作为承运人签署单据的证据”这样的规定。

［原文］Article 25　Courier Receipt, Post Receipt or Certificate of Posting

a. A courier receipt, however named, evidencing receipt of goods for transport, must appear to:

i. indicate the name of the courier service and be stamped or signed by the named courier service at the place from which the credit states the goods are to be shipped; and

ii. indicate a date of pick-up or of receipt or wording to this effect. This date will be deemed to be the date of shipment.

b. A requirement that courier charges are to be paid or prepaid may be satisfied by a transport document issued by a courier service evidencing that courier charges are for the account of a party other than the consignee.

c. A post receipt or certificate of posting, however named, evidencing receipt of goods for transport, must appear to be stamped or signed and dated at the place from which the credit states the goods are to be shipped. This date will be deemed to be the date of shipment.

[译文] 第二十五条　快递收据、邮政收据和投递证明

a. 不论称谓如何，证明货物收讫待运的快递收据，必须在表面看来：

i. 注明快递机构的名称，并在信用证规定的货物发运地点由该具名快递机构盖章或签字；并且

ii. 注明取件或收件的日期或同义词语，此日期即视为装运日期。

b. 如果信用证要求快递费用付讫或预付，则快递机构出具的证实快递费由收货人以外的一方承担的运输单据可以符合该项要求。

c. 不论如何称谓，表明货物收讫待运的邮政收据或投递证明，必须在表面看来由信用证规定的货物装运地点盖章或签署且注明日期。该日期将被视为装运日期。

[讲解]

1. 当货物采用快递方式寄送时，则由快递机构签发“快递收据”（courier receipt）。当采用一般邮寄方式寄送货物时，则由邮寄签发“邮政收据”（post receipt），也称作“包裹单”。至于“投递证明”（certificate of posting），则是由投递机构如邮局开具的、证明已收到货物待发运的一种证明单据。

2. 快递费用的支付，应当与贸易术语相结合。如采用CPT或CIP贸易术语时，有关快递单据上应表明快递费“付讫”/“预付”字样，表示快递费用由收货人以外的一方承担。

3. 无论“快递收据”或“邮政收据”，都不代表货物所有权，也不是提货的依据。货物运抵目的地后，快递机构/邮局或将货物送到单上列明的收货人处，或向收货人发出“到货通知”，由收货人持“到货通知”和证明身份的证件到快递机构/邮局提取货物。实际上发货人将货物交付快递机构/邮局后，已经丧失了对货物的控制权。为此，发货人在缮制信用证规定的单据时，要特别注意，避免货物运抵目的地已被提走，而由于收汇单据的差错形成单证不符，以致丧失银行的付款保证，造成货款落空的风险。

［与第500号出版物比较］

本条增加“投递证明”、快递费何方支付等内容。其他内容基本与第500号出版物的第二十八条类似。

［原文］ Article 26 "On Deck", "Shipper's Load and Count", "Said by Shipper to Contain" and Charges Additional to Freight

a. A transport document must not indicate that the goods are or will be loaded on deck. A clause on a transport document stating that the goods may be loaded on deck is acceptable.

b. A transport document bearing a clause such as "shipper's load and count" and "said by shipper to contain" is acceptable.

c. A transport document may bear a reference, by stamp or otherwise, to charges additional to the freight.

[译文] 第二十六条 "货装舱面"、"托运人装载并计数"、"内容据托运人报称"及运费以外的附加费用

a. 运输单据不得注明货物已装或者将装于舱面。运输单据条款中注明货物可能被装于舱面，银行将予以接受。

b. 含有诸如"托运人装载并计数"或"内容据托运人报称"条款的运输单据，银行将予以接受。

c. 运输单据上可以包含以印章或其他方式提及运费以外的附加费用。

[讲解]

1. 本条从以下几方面对运输单据做了明确的规定。首先是"货装舱面"的问题。木条规定"运输单据不得注明货物装于或者将装于舱面"，"声明货物可能被装于舱面的运输条款可以接受"。笔者认为，这样的规定，无疑是正确的。因为，当今用于国际贸易货物的包装，除了单件运输包装外，还有集合运输包装。单件运输包装，如木箱、纸箱、筐、篓、麻包等，由于受自身条件所限，如果存放在舱面，极易受风吹、浪打、日晒和雨淋的侵袭，致使货物受到损失。所以银行不能接受"货物已装或者将装舱面"的运输单据。至于货物装入集合运输包装的集装箱，则情况另当别论。因为集装箱能防水防晒，本身既大又重，不可能装在舱内（少数集装箱堆放在舱内），如果硬性规定不能装于舱面，这显然是不对的，也不可能做到。所以本条又规定"声明货物可能被装于舱面的运输单据，可以'被银行'接受"。

2. 本条又规定银行接受注有"托运人装载和计数"、"内容据托运人报称"等条款的运输单据。笔者认为：这是结合业务实际制定的惯例，也是银行务实的做法。因为承运人无法逐笔清点每位托运人所托运货物的数量和件数，也无法了解托运人所托运货物的实际内容（除非逐件打开包装清点，实际上也做不到）。

单件运输包装的货物如此，集合运输包装的货物也是如此。所以，各种运输单据——“海洋提单”、“承运货物收据”以及“国际铁路联运运单”等，基本上都注明“货物细目由托运人提供”、“托运人提供的详细情况”及“货物的内容、数量、重量及体积由托运人提供”等词句。本条的规定，解决了银行和运输方对某些问题认识不一致情况。

3. 运输单据上，除了记载运费外，是否还可以记载其他费用，如集装箱码头使用费、拼箱费及拆箱费等。对此问题，一直存在不同意见，本条规定可以记载，这样就统一了认识，也便于实际操作。

［与第500号出版物比较］

本条与第500号出版物的第三十一条内容相似。由于前面有关运输方式的几条内，已经规定允许第三方作为发货人，所在本条内删去第500号出版物的第三十一条内有关发货人的内容。增添允许在运输单据上加注除运费以外的其他费用的规定。

［原文］**Article 27　Clean Transport Document**

A bank will only accept a clean transport document. A clean transport document is one bearing no clause or notation expressly declaring a defective condition of the goods or their packaging. The word “clean” need not appear on a transport document, even if a credit has a requirement for that transport document to be “clean on board”.

［译文］第二十七条　清洁运输单据

银行只接受清洁运输单据。清洁运输单据系指未载有明确宣称货物或包装有缺陷的条款或批注的运输单据。即使信用证要求“清洁已装船”的运输单据，运输单据也无须出现“清洁”字样。

［讲解］

1. 本条是专门为“清洁”运输单据而规定的。在所有的结算单据中，运输单据有其独特的重要性。因为有的运输单据如海运指示提单（order B/L）和空白提单（open B/L）等都代表货物所有权，能转让流通。有的运输单据如航空运单及邮政收据等，虽不能提取货物，但也作为结算货款的重要依据。所以，是否是“清洁”运输单据，就显得特别重要。什么是“清洁运输单据”？按本条规定：清洁运输单据系指未载有明确宣称货物或包装有缺陷条款或批注的运输单据。例如，运输单据加载有“xx 件损坏”（xx packages in damaged condition），“被雨淋湿”（rain wet）等，这就成为不清洁运输单据，如果是海运提单，便成为“不清洁提单”（unclean B/L or foul B/L）。应该指出的是：虽然惯例对构成“不清洁运输单据”的条件规定比较明确，但这种概念并非被普遍接受。有的人士还认为：只要运输单据上有承运人 / 代理对货物或包装加了批注，便构成“不清洁运输单据”，进而影响出口人收回货款。这种认识或做法，显然是不对的。国际海运公会（International Chamber of Shipping）认为海运提单上即使有以上批注，仍旧不算是“不清洁提单”。

（1）不明确表示货物或包装有不能令人满意的批注。如“旧箱”、“旧桶”及“旧麻袋”等。这种认识无疑是正确的。因为货物使用“旧箱”或“旧桶”包装，这极可能就是交易条件之一，有了这种批注的单据，并不已经成为“不清洁”的运输单据。如果单据上批注的词句是“旧麻袋包装，数个已破”，这就意味已经不属于成交条件了，因为破包装已经直接影响货物的质量，提单当然就成为“不清洁提单”了。

（2）强调承运人对货物或包装性质所引起的风险不负责任的批注。如出口黄磷装在充水的铁桶内，如果在运输过程中，桶内的水消失，造成黄磷自燃而灭失。货到目的港卸货时，只剩空桶而无货物，承运人对此不负责任。为此，承运人在提单上注明以上词句，避免承担责任。提单上虽有这种批注，也不能算作“不清洁提单”。

（3）否认承运人知道货物的内容、重量、容量、质量或技术条件的批注。承运人如果要想了解所装货物的具体情况，必须逐件打开检查、称重量。实际上这是做不到的。所以承运人在提单上才有如上批注，借以分清责任。

据了解，国际海运公会的这些解释，已被众多家银行认可和接受。笔者认为：本条规定与国际海运公会的解释并不矛盾，是互为补充，更加便于执行。

2. 由于不清洁运输单据对货款的回收影响甚大，所以托运人（供货方）要对出现不清洁运输单据严加防范。在货物装运前，必须切实检查货物的质量和包装，无论货物是集装箱装运或采用单件运输包装。一旦发现货物本身或包装有破损、有“跑冒滴漏”现象时，要立即采取紧急措施，加以补救。杜绝承运人/代理签发不清洁运输单据。

［与第500号出版物比较］

本条与第500号出版物的第三十二条内容基本相似，但本条强调“只接受……”，严格规定“清洁运输单据”的要点。本条删除了旧条款中“除非信用证规定可以接受……”的词句。从字面理解，可以说没有迴旋余地。因此，对什么是“不清洁运输单据”，一定要掌握确切，避免发生差错而造成经济上的损失。

［原文］Article 28　Insurance Document and Coverage

a. An insurance document, such as an insurance policy, an insurance certificate or a declaration under an open cover, must appear to be issued and signed by an insurance company, an underwriter or their agents or their proxies.

Any signature by an agent or proxy must indicate whether the agent or proxy has signed for or on behalf of the insurance company or underwriter.

b. When the insurance document indicates that it has been issued in more than one original, all originals must be presented.

c. Cover notes will not be accepted.

d. An insurance policy is acceptable in lieu of an insurance certificate or a declaration under an open cover.

e. The date of the insurance document must be no later than the date of shipment, unless it appears from the insurance document that the cover is effective from a date not later than the date of shipment.

f. i. The insurance document must indicate the amount of insurance coverage and be in the same currency as the credit.

ii. A requirement in the credit for insurance coverage to be for a percentage of the value of the goods, of the invoice value or similar is deemed to be the minimum amount of coverage required.

If there is no indication in the credit of the insurance coverage required, the amount of insurance coverage must be at least 110% of the CIF or CIP value of the goods.

When the CIF or CIP value cannot be determined from the documents, the amount of insurance coverage must be calculated on the basis of the amount for which honour or negotiation is requested or the gross value of the goods as shown on the invoice, whichever is greater.

iii. The insurance document must indicate that risks are covered at least between the place of taking in charge or shipment and the place of discharge or final destination as stated in the credit.

g. A credit should state the type of insurance required and, if any, the additional risks to be covered. An insurance document will be accepted without regard to any risks that are not covered if the credit uses imprecise terms such as "usual risks" or "customary risks".

h. When a credit requires insurance against "all risks" and an insurance document is presented containing any "all risks" notation or clause, whether or not bearing the heading "all risks", the insurance document will be accepted without regard to any risks stated to be excluded.

i. An insurance document may contain reference to any exclusion clause.

j. An insurance document may indicate that the cover is subject to a franchise or excess (deductible).

[译文] 第二十八条　保险单据及保险责任范围

a. 保险单据，诸如保险单或预保单项下的保险证明或者保险声明，必须在表面看来由保险公司、承保人或他们的代理和代表出具并签署。

代理或代表的签字必须表明其是代表保险公司或承保人签署。

b. 如果保险单据表明所出具正本单据系一份以上，则必须提交全部正本保险单据。

c. 银行将不接受暂保单。

d. 银行可以接受保险单取代预保单项下的保险证明或保险声明。

e. 除非保险单据表明保险责任不迟于装运日生效，则保险单据签发日期不得晚于装运日期。

f. i. 保险单据必须注明投保金额并使用与信用证相同的货币出具。

ii. 信用证中关于投保金额为货物价值、发票金额或类似金额的一定比例的要求，应视为对最低保额的要求。

如果信用证中未规定投保金额，则投保金额至少为货物 CIF

或 CIP 价格的 110%。

如果从单据中不能确定 CIF 或者 CIP 价格，投保金额必须基于信用证要求付款或议付的金额，或者发票上显示的货物总值来计算，两者之中取金额较高者。

iii. 保险单据注明的保险责任范围应至少包括从信用证规定的货物监管地或装运地开始到卸货地或最终目的地为止。

g. 信用证应规定所需投保的险别种类以及附加险别（如有)。如果信用证使用诸如“通常险别”或“惯常险别”等意义不明确的条款，则无论是否漏保任何险别，保险单据将被照样接受。

h. 当信用证要求投保“一切险”时，只要保险单据含有任何“一切险”批注或条款，不论其是否有“一切险”标题，甚至表明不包括某些险别，均将被接受。

i. 保险单据可以援引任何免责条款 。

j. 保险单据可以注明受免赔率或免赔额（减除额）约束。

[讲解]

1. 本条规定，签发保险单据的签发人，不仅有经常见到的承保人或他们的代理，新增加承保人的代表（proxy）也可签发保险单据。由此可见保险业务日益增长。

2. 明确规定银行不接受暂保单（cover notes)。规定银行接受保险单以代替预保单项下的保险证明或者保险声明。

3. 本条之所以规定“除非保险单据表明保险责任不迟于装运日生效，否则保险单据签发日不得晚于装运日”。笔者认为，这是根据货物的特点及保险责任条款来考虑的。货物运输保险中基本险别的责任起讫，世界上普遍采用“仓至仓条款”（warehouse to warehouse clause)，即货物离开保险单据所注明的启（装）运地发货人仓库后，保险责任开始生效，直至货物进入保险单据上所注明的卸货地收货人仓库后，保险责任便告结束。如果保险单据的签发日晚于装运日期，前一个“仓”就不能起到作用。所以规定保险单据的签发日期不得晚于装运日期是很正确的。但是，有的散装货物，如煤、焦炭和矿砂等，一般采用传送带或抓斗将货物装上运输工具，必须在装完后才能知悉装载重量，才能出具保险单据。所以，保险单据上可以根据货物的特殊情况，表明保险责任不迟于装运日期生效，这样的处理方式，是可以接受的。

4. 当出口货物采用 CIP、CIP 以及 DES、DEQ 等贸易术语，进口货物采用 FOB、FAS、CFR 和 CPT 贸易术语时，就会涉及货物的保险问题。关于投保金额，本条规定投保人按 CIF /CIP 货值的 110%投保，也就是投保加一成。这一成就是投保人的预期利润和费用。如果由于贸易上的原因，当事人不愿在单据上显示所使用的贸易术语时，只能根据要求银行付款金额或者银行议付金额，或商业发票上注明的总货值，取其高者作为投保金额。

5. 本条严格规定投保所使用的币别，要与信用证内的币别一致。笔者认为：这项规定，既考虑到保险机构在理赔时由于币别不同而引起在折算方面的困难，也杜绝投保人在投保时对不同货币币值升/降的投机做法。

6. 如果信用证规定投保“一切险”时，本条规定，只要保险单据内含有任何有关“一切险”的批注或条款，便可满足要求。但应注意：现在国际贸易通用的货物运输保险条款有三种：“中国保险条款”（China Insurance Clauses，CIC）、“英国伦敦协会货物保险条款”（Institute Cargo Clauses，ICC）和“美国协会货物条款”（American Institute Cargo Clauses，AICC）。CIC 和 AICC 都有“一切险”的名称，但 ICC 没有“一切险”，只有责任范围大体上和“一切险”相当的“协会货物条款（A）”[ICC（A）]。笔者认为，在课堂或书刊上介绍不同险别条款时，可以介绍“一切险”的责任范围和“协会货物（A）条款”大体上相同。但在保险单据上却不能出现这种含糊而不确定的词句。实际上，两种险别在承保范围方面，还是存在不少区别。因此，如来证规定保险“按协会条款投保一切险”时，以要求对方改为协会条款的险别为宜。

7. 一切易损货物，在保险单上经常注明“免赔率”。这是指货物在运输过程中遭受损失时，如损失在一定的百分数范围内，保险机构可以免予赔偿。应该注意的是，免赔率分“相对免赔率”（franchise）和“绝对免赔率”（deductible）两种。当货物遭受承保范围内的损失，如损失超过规定免赔率，采用“相对免赔率”时，则不用扣除免赔率，全部予以赔偿。用采用“绝对免赔率”时，则须扣除免赔率，只赔偿超过部分。例如，出口一批易损货物——平板玻璃，投保金额为 USD 100 000，免赔率为 3%。货物运抵目的地后，经检查，部分玻璃破碎，损失达 USD 5 000，破损率达 5%，已超过 3% 免赔率。在计算赔偿金额时，如采用“相对免赔率”，保险机构不用扣除免赔率，应赔付投保人 USD 5 000。如采用“绝对免赔率”，保险机构应赔偿：5%（USD 5 000）－3%（USD 3 000）＝2%（USD 2 000）

为了便于理赔时计算赔偿金额和有依据，本条规定：允许保险单据上注明“免赔率”或“免赔额”，为计算赔偿时提供方便，无疑是很恰当的。

[与第 500 号出版物比较]

本条与第 500 号出版物的第三十四、三十五和三十六条内容相似。但本条增加允许承保人的代表，作为保险单据的签发人。

[原文] Article 29　Extension of Expiry Date or Last Day for Presentation

a. If the expiry date of a credit or the last day for presentation falls on a day when the bank to which presentation is to be made is closed for reasons other than those referred to in article 36, the expiry date or the last day for presentation, as the case may be, will be extended to the first following banking day.

b. If presentation is made on the first following banking day, a nominated bank must provide the issuing bank or confirming bank with a statement on its covering schedule that the presentation was made within the time limits extended in accordance with sub-article 29 (a).

c. The latest date for shipment will not be extended as a result of sub-article 29 (a).

[译文] 第二十九条　到期日或最迟交单日的顺延

a. 如果信用证的到期日或最迟交单日适逢接受单据的银行因第三十六条条款以外的原因而中止营业，则到期日或最迟交单日，将根据具体情况顺延至该银行开业的第一个营业日。

b. 如果在顺延后的第一个营业日交单，则指定银行必须向开证行或保兑行申明交单系根据第二十九条 a 款规定的顺延期限内所提交。

c. 最迟装运日不因第二十九条 a 款规定的原因而顺延。

[讲解]

1. 本条指出：如果信用证的到期日或最后交单日适逢银行因不可抗力以外的原因而停止营业，则可以将该两种日期延长到银行重新营业的第一个营业日为止。这个掌握日期的方法，对于装运期不适用。例如一份信用证规定有效期是 6 月 28 日，装运期不得晚于 6 月 25 日。在货物未装出前，6 月 20 日银行因一些特殊原因而停止营业。6 月 30 日银行恢复营业，该证有效期可以延至 30 日当天，但装运期不能顺延。由于货物没在 6 月 25 日前及当天装出，本证已超过装运期，不能再装运。

2. 如果受益人按照上述情况向（出口地）银行交付单据，后者在寄单时，应该向开证行/保兑行书面声明单据确实在银行恢复营业后第一个营业日交付的。这样做的目的，是为了避免开证行/保兑行误认受益人超过规定时间交单而拒付货款，致使受益人遭受经济上的损失。

[与第 500 号出版物比较]

本条与第 500 号出版物的第三十四条的内容相似。

[原文] Article 30 Tolerance in Credit Amount, Quantity and Unit Prices

a. The words "about" or "approximately" used in connection with the amount of the credit or the quantity or the unit price stated in the credit are to be construed as allowing a tolerance not to exceed 10% more or 10% less than the amount, the quantity or the unit price to which they refer.

b. A tolerance not to exceed 5% more or 5% less than the quantity of the goods is allowed, provided the credit does not state the quantity in terms of a stipulated number of packing units or individual items and the total amount of the drawings does not exceed the amount of the credit.

c. Even when partial shipments are not allowed, a tolerance not to exceed 5% less than the amount of the credit is allowed, provided that the quantity of the goods, if stated in the credit, is shipped in full and a unit price, if stated in the credit, is not reduced or that sub-article 30 (b) is not applicable. This tolerance does not apply when the credit stipulates a specific tolerance or uses the expressions referred to in sub-article 30 (a).

[译文] 第三十条 信用证金额、数量和单价的增减幅度

a. "约"或"大约"用于信用证规定金额、数量或单价时，应解释为允许有关金额、数量或单价不超过 10% 的增减幅度。

b. 只要信用证未注明货物以包装单位或个数计数，并且总支付金额不超过信用证金额，货物数量准许有5%的增减幅度。

c. 如果信用证规定了货物数量，且该数量已全部发运，以及当信用证对单价有规定，而此单价又未降低时，或者当第三十条b款不适用时，则即使不允许部分装运，也允许支取的金额有5%的减幅。若信用证规定特定的增减幅度或者使用第三十条a款提到的用语限定数量，则该减幅不适用。

［讲解］

1. 对于信用证内货物的金额、数量和单价的前面注有“约”(about)/“大约”（approximately）的文字时，金额、数量和单价均有10%的增减幅度。如 about100 M/T @ USD100 per M/T total amount about USD10 000。由于数量和总值前都有“约”字，按本条规定，这批货物最多可装出110 M/T——USD11 000 最少不能少于90 M/T——USD90 000。另一方面，如果数量和金额前没有“约”字，或者数量/金额中，只有一项前有“约”字：

（1）如果信用证中没有规定货物的数量不得增减；

（2）支取金额不超过证内金额；

（3）货物不是以包、箱、件、打等包装单位/个数单位来计价。如果符合以上三条规定，则允许交货数量及金额有5%的增减幅度。

2. “货物的单价不变，数量没有分批，一次装出。允许发货人支取的金额，有5%的减幅”。本条的这项规定，看起来似乎不大容易理解，其实，在实际业务中，完全有可能出现来证金额大于卖方回收款项的现象。如开证人（买方）在开出的信用证的总金额中，除货款外，还增加偿还受益人（卖方）代为租船订舱的运费、代为投保的保险费和有关装运费用等。例如，当卖方以FOB/FAS贸易术语出口货物，买方在当地租船订舱有困难，遂委托卖方代为办理此项工作。允诺将来卖方代为垫付的运费和货款一并从信用证中扣除。由于开证时舱位尚未订妥，因此，运费及有关装运费用是估计的。货物装出后，实际运费已经算出，因此收回的货款及运费，一般要比来证金额小（来证金额稍大于实际支付金额）。又如：卖方以 CFR/CPT 贸易术语出口货物，由于各种原因，买方委托卖方代为投保。卖方所垫付的保险费将来在结算货款时一并归还。但由于保险费率一般不公开，所以来证总金额中包括的保险费，也会比实际支付的要大些。由于以上诸种原因，所以惯例制定本条内容。即允许回收的款项，可以有比证内金额少 5%的幅度。这项规定，既可以便于买/卖双方遵照执行，也避免卖方在回收款项时由于与银行看法不一致而影响正常收汇工作。

［与第 500 号出版物比较］

本条与第 500 号出版物的第三十九条相似，但旧惯例规定：凡“约”（about）、“大概”（approximately）、“大约”（circa）或类似的词语，用于信用证金额、数量……新惯例做以下规定：“约”（about）或“大概”（approximately）用于信用证金额或信用证规定的数量、单价时……新旧条款相比，后者删去了“大约”（circa）和“或类似的词语”。所以，在实际业务中要特别注意，遇到证内有类似词句时，一定要加强出口单位内部研究、银贸研究（即征求银行的意见），力求取得共识。特别强调要等到银贸双方的意见取得一致后，才去执行。

［原文］Article 31 Partial Drawings or Shipments

a. Partial drawings or shipments are allowed.

b. A presentation consisting of more than one set of transport documents evidencing shipment commencing on the same means of conveyance and for the same journey, provided they indicate the same destination, will not be regarded as covering a partial shipment, even if they indicate different dates of shipment or different ports of loading, places of taking in charge or dispatch. If the presentation consists of more than one set of transport documents, the latest date of shipment as evidenced on any of the sets of transport documents will be regarded as the date of shipment.

A presentation consisting of one or more sets of transport documents evidencing shipment on more than one means of conveyance within the same mode of transport will be regarded as covering a partial shipment, even if the means of conveyance leave on the same day for the same destination.

c. A presentation consisting of more than one courier receipt, post receipt or certificate of posting will not be regarded as a partial shipment if the courier receipts, post receipts or certificates of posting appear to have been stamped or signed by the same courier or postal service at the same place and date and for the same destination.

[译文] 第三十一条　分批支款或分批装运

a. 允许分批支款或分批装运。

b. 提交的数套运输单据中表明货物系使用同一运输工具并经由同一路线运输，即使运输单据上注明的装运日期不同或装货港、接受监管地、发运地点不同，只要注明的目的地相同，将不视为分批装运。如果提交的单据由数套运输单据构成，在所有单据中注明的最迟一个发运日将被视为装运日。

即使运输工具在同一天出发并开往同一目的地，只要提交的数套运输单据中表明货物系在同一种运输方式下使用不止一个运输工具运输，则将被视为分批装运。

c. 如果所提交的单据在表面看来由同一地点的快递机构或邮政机构在同一日期加盖印章或签署并且发往同一目的地，则提交一份以上快递收据、邮政收据或投递证明将不视为分批装运。

[讲解]

1. 本条对分批支款和分批装运做了仔细和明确的规定，在通常情况下，信用证受益人收款金额的大小，是根据所发运货物的数量来决定的。但也有个别例外情况。有的信用证内规定：可以分批装运，但不能分批支用款项。如某单位向国外出口全套设备，由于设备体积庞大，部件众多，生产厂家生产出一批零部件后就发运到对方，同时提交一批单据，但不能支取部分货款。直到全部设备发运完毕，才支付全部设备款项（也有的待设备试车成功后/试生产合格后才付款）。有的信用证可以分批支用款项，但没有分批装运。如开证人为了支付租金、劳务费或还款而向对方开出备用信用证，允许受益人分批支用款项。但由于没有货物，所以就不存在分批装运的问题。总之，如信用证内如果没有特别规定，就意味该证允许分批装运和分批支款。

2. 凡是用同一运输工具，同一个航次，运往相同的目的地。即使在不同的地点发运，最后将数套运输单据集中，一起交付银行。这样做并不构成“分批”。例如，天津 A 出口公司有一份发往伦敦 200 吨货物的信用证。证内规定必须一次装出，不得分批装运（partial shipments are not allowed），装运期为 7 月份（shipment during July）。A 公司在天津只有 50 吨货，其余分别在青岛和大连。如果将外地的 150 吨货物运往天津，集中 200 吨装出，势必增加不少由大连及青岛运往天津的运费。为了节省费用，A 公司采用分别在大连、天津和青岛装船的办法。7 月 25 日在青岛装上同一航次“友谊”号班轮 70 吨货物，目的港为伦敦。7 月 27 日在天津新港将 50 吨货装上同一航次“友谊”号轮，目的港为伦敦。7 月 29 日同一航次“友谊”号轮在大连装货 80 吨，目的港也是伦敦。这三处分别装货的三套提单共计 200 吨，最后一次在大连的装运日为 7 月 29 日，没有超过信用证规定的装运期。提单集中天津后，连同其他信用证规定的单据，一并送交银行。这种做法，符合证内要求，不算“分批”。

3. 以第2点为例。如货物分别在三地装船，货物在青岛和天津都分别装上同一航次“友谊”号轮船，当船到大连时，由于当地待装货物很多，托运人订不到“友谊”号轮船的舱位，不得已只好改订另一艘船“胜利”号舱位。三地装货的目的港都是伦敦。全部单据最后也集中天津交单，装运期也没有超过信用证规定的装运期限。但由于使用了不同的运输工具（货物装在两艘不同船名的船上），按本条规定，算作“分批”装运。

4. 当货物采用“快递”、“邮包”方式发运时，由于这两种方式对货物的单件长度、重量均有限制。如托运的货物较多时，就不得不分成若干包/件发送。本条对这种情况也做出相应规定：只要在相同地点和相同日期发送，并且货物运往的目的地也相同，即使发送单位出具多份“快递收据”或“邮政收据”或“投递证明”，也不算作“分批”。

[与第500号出版物比较]

本条与第500号出版物的第四十条内容基本相似。

[原文] **Article 32　Instalment Drawings or Shipments**

If a drawing or shipment by instalments within given periods is stipulated in the credit and any instalment is not drawn or shipped within the period allowed for that instalment, the credit ceases to be available for that and any subsequent instalment.

[译文] 第三十二条　分期支款或分期装运

信用证规定的在特定期限内分期支款或分期装运，如果其中任何一期未按信用证所规定期限支款或装运，则信用证对该期及以后各期均视为无效。

[讲解]

1. 本条所规定的内容，与上条不一样。本条是指在规定的时间内分几次支取货款或者在规定的时间内分几次发运货物。如果受益人在其中任何一期未按信用证规定去做，那么，自该期和以后的各期规定也就失去作用。例如，信用证规定受益人在 1—6 月每月装运出口货物 100 吨，开证行根据每次发出货物的单据予以偿付货款。受益人在 1、2、3 月份每月按规定发出 100 吨货物，每次发货后，均凭单据结算货款。4 月份因货源紧张，没有发货。5 月份继续发货，装出 200 吨，结果遭到银行拒付。同样，原规定 6 月份要发出 100 吨货物的安排，也因 4 月份未发货而宣告中止。

2. 至于上例中受益人已经取得了 1、2、3 月份发出货物的货款，如何处理问题，是退还是不退？开证人是否索赔？这属买卖之间的商业纠纷，由双方自行处理，银行对此不再参与。

[与第 500 号出版物比较]

本条与第 500 号出版物的第四十一条的内容基本相同，但本条删除了原第四十一条中“信用证另有规定者除外”这样的词句，也就是排除了允许有“例外”的情况

[原文] **Article 33　Hours of Presentation**

A bank has no obligation to accept a presentation outside of its banking hours.

[译文] 第三十三条　交单时间

银行在其营业时间外，无接受提交单据的义务。

[讲解]

本条规定：信用证当事人向银行交付单据，必须在银行的营业时间进行。因此，交单时间就显得尤为重要。因为，如果当事人在信用证规定的时间、规定的地点，向银行交出符合信用证规定的单据，便可以顺利收到款项。例如，出口商A公司收到一份装运期为10月8日、有效期为10月15日，在受益人所在地到期的限定议付信用证。该公司装完货后，备齐信用证内规定的各种单据，经审核正确无误后，于15日前，甚至15日当天银行营业时间内，送交当地的指定银行。这样做是符合信用证规定的。如果该证规定10月15日在开证人所在地到期，由开证行审单付款，则受益人必须仔细计算邮寄时间，提前将全套单据通过当地银行（非信用证指定银行）向开证行寄出。单据务必在信用证有效期到期前/当天的银行营业时间内到达开证行。否则，即使单据内容正确无误，但由于单据到达时间已超过信用证规定的有效期，这笔货款将失去银行信用的保障。

[与第500号出版物比较]

本条和第500号出版物的第四十五条内容基本相同。

[原文] **Article 34　Disclaimer on Effectiveness of Documents**

A bank assumes no liability or responsibility for the form, sufficiency, accuracy, genuineness, falsification or legal effect of any document, or for the general or particular conditions stipulated in a document or superimposed thereon; nor does it assume any liability or responsibility for the description, quantity, weight, quality, condition, packing, delivery, value or existence of the goods, services or other performance represented by any document, or for the good faith or acts or omissions, solvency, performance or standing of the consignor, the carrier, the forwarder, the consignee or the insurer of the goods or any other person.

[译文] 第三十四条　对单据有效性的免责

银行对任何单据的形式、完整性、准确性、内容真实性、单据真伪性或法律效力，或对于单据中规定的或附加的一般性或特殊性条件，概不负责；银行对于任何单据所代表的货物、服务和其他履约行为的描述、数量、重量、质量、状况、包装、交货、价值或存在，对于发货人、承运人、货运代理人、收货人、保险承保人或其他任何人的诚信、行为、疏忽、清偿能力、履约能力和信誉状况，也概不负责。

[讲解]

1. 本条主要用文字表明银行对于信用证当事人提交的单据，承担 /不承担责任的范围。银行审核单据，主要看单据的表面，是否与信用证的规定或要求相符。“单单一致”、“单证（信用证）一致”是银行对单据的要求。至于单据的形式、内容是否充分、是否虚假伪造，银行对此无法掌握也不能承担责任。例如以商业发票为例，这种单据种类众多，哪一种式样的商业发票内容齐备、项目充分？谁也说不清楚。所以，银行对商业发票的形式、内容不便掌握，只要这种单据上注有“商业发票”字样，便符合信用证的基本要求。至于发票内对货物、服务或其他方面的描述，银行不予掌握。应特别注意的是：凡信用证要求在商业发票上表明的内容，必须照办。否则，便形成单、证不符的现象。

2. 信用证受益人提交给银行的各种单据中，涉及不少各方面的有关当事人，如发货人、收货人、承运人、货运代理人（货代）、货物的保险人等。银行对他们的资信、偿付能力及信誉情况等方面，是不承担责任的。

[与第 500 号出版物比较]

本条与第 500 号出版物的第十五条的内容基本相同。

［原文］**Article 35　Disclaimer on Transmission and Translation**

A bank assumes no liability or responsibility for the consequences arising out of delay, loss in transit, mutilation or other errors arising in the transmission of any messages or delivery of letters or documents, when such messages, letters or documents are transmitted or sent according to the requirements stated in the credit, or when the bank may have taken the initiative in the choice of the delivery service in the absence of such instructions in the credit.

If a nominated bank determines that a presentation is complying and forwards the documents to the issuing bank or confirming bank, whether or not the nominated bank has honoured or negotiated, an issuing bank or confirming bank must honour or negotiate, or reimburse that nominated bank, even when the documents have been lost in transit between the nominated bank and the issuing bank or confirming bank, or between the confirming bank and the issuing bank.

A bank assumes no liability or responsibility for errors in translation or interpretation of technical terms and may transmit credit terms without translating them.

［译文］**第三十五条　关于信息传递和翻译的免责**

当报文、信件或单据按照信用证的要求传递或发送，或者当信用证未作规定而银行主动选择传递机构时，银行对任何报文、信函或单据的传递过程中发生的延误、途中丢失、残缺或其他错误产生的后果，概不负责。

如果指定银行确定提示相符且将单据寄往开证行或保兑行，不论指定银行是否已经付款或议付，即使单据在指定银行寄往开证行或保兑行的途中，或保兑行寄往开证行的途中丢失，则开证行或保兑行必须付款、议付，或者偿付指定银行。

银行对技术术语的笔译和口译中错误不负责任，并可不加翻译地照转信用证原文。

[讲解]

1. 本条强调银行（通常情况下是通知行）将信用证传递给受益人时，是原文照转，不加翻译。因为翻译件容易产生差错。

2. 出口地银行将审核过的单据寄往开证行，无论是按照来证指示办理寄送，或来证没有具体指示要求，仅由出口地银行自行选择寄送方式寄送，一旦单据发生破损、丢失或短缺现象，寄单行不承担责任。笔者认为：一旦单据发生上述情况的损失，银行基本可以不承担责任。但应对出现的事件，要做具体分析，以明确责任究竟应由何方承担，至少还可以吸取教训，引以为戒。如某地 H 贸易公司，根据国外开来的信用证，办理了发货、装船工作后，将信用证内规定的单据送交出口地 T 银行。T 银行对该套单据进行了审核，没有发现差错，便准备将单据寄国外开证行索取款项。该份信用证内对寄单方法只注明："单据分两批（two lots）寄交开证行"。T 银行的工作人员在寄单时，将所有包括提单、保险单在内的单据正本，集中在一起，一次寄出。另将一套全是副本的单据，也一次寄出。不巧，单据在寄送途中办理转运飞机航班手续时，内装正本单据的邮包不慎丢失。开证行只收到全套副本单据。由于没有正本单据，开证行无法将单据交付申请人，也就无法结算本信用证已装出货物的款项。同时，也由于没有正本提单，造成开证人无法提货。这件事发生后，T 银行的工作人员强调"惯例"上有明文规定。因而不承认应该对此事负有责任。笔者认为，T 银行的工作人员，不能引用惯例上有相应规定而开脱自己。相反，该工作人员要承担单据丢失的责任。因为来证指定单据要分两批寄出，就是考虑到单据在寄送途中有可能丢失。既然如此，银行寄单时就应该把正本单据分装两处，分别寄出，以免丢失，这是一般常识。如果两套单据在运送途中全部丢失，还可以考虑援引“惯例”来免除寄单银行的责任。现在情况不是这样，寄单人把所有正本单据放在一起，一次寄出，而把所有副本单据放在另外一包内寄出。结果恰恰是装有正本单据的邮包丢失。所以，该人员不能推脱应承担的责任。而开证行由于没有收到全套单据，自然不能承担付款义务。

［与第 500 号出版物比较］

本条的内容和第 500 号出版物的第十六条基本相同。但有的地方规定更明确、便于执行，如对单据在寄送途中丢失的处理，银行对技术翻译承担的责任等。

［原文］ **Article 36　Force Majeure**

A bank assumes no liability or responsibility for the consequences arising out of the interruption of its business by Acts of God, riots, civil commotions, insurrections, wars, acts of terrorism, or by any strikes or lockouts or any other causes beyond its control.

A bank will not, upon resumption of its business, honour or negotiate under a credit that expired during such interruption of its business.

［译文］ 第三十六条　不可抗力

银行对于天灾、暴动、骚乱、叛乱、战争、恐怖主义行为或任何罢工、停工或银行本身无法控制的任何其他原因所导致的中断营业的后果，概不负责。

银行在恢复营业后，对于在中断营业期间已逾期的信用证，将不再据以付款或议付。

［讲解］

1. 在进出口贸易业务过程中，经常会碰到一些不是由于交易方的原因造成的意外事件，致使贸易活动受到影响，甚至因此而夭折。对于不可抗力的含义、范围及对事故的处理，不少书刊、贸易合同对此也有一些规定，大体都把不可抗力条款分成三类：概括式规定、列举式规定和综合式规定。这三种规定方法各有所长，也各有所短，总感到不十分满意。笔者认为：本条规定明确、简捷，易于理解，便于执行。

2. 本条在列举造成不可抗力事故的诸多因素中，还包括“恐怖主义”，这是结合危害当今世界和平生活的一大毒瘤而列入的，非常及时。

[与第 500 号出版物比较]

本条内容与第 500 号出版物的第十七条基本相同。本条新将“恐怖主义”列入不可抗力的因素。

[原文] Article 37　Disclaimer for Acts of an Instructed Party

a. A bank utilizing the services of another bank for the purpose of giving effect to the instructions of the applicant does so for the account and at the risk of the applicant.

b. An issuing bank or advising bank assumes no liability or responsibility should the instructions it transmits to another bank not be carried out, even if it has taken the initiative in the choice of that other bank.

c. A bank instructing another bank to perform services is liable for any commissions, fees, costs or expenses (“charges”) incurred by that bank in connection with its instructions. If a credit states that charges are for the account of the beneficiary and charges cannot be collected or deducted from proceeds, the issuing bank remains liable for payment of charges.

A credit or amendment should not stipulate that the advising to a beneficiary is conditional upon the receipt by the advising bank or second advising bank of its charges.

d. The applicant shall be bound by and liable to indemnify a bank against all obligations and responsibilities imposed by foreign laws and usages.

［译文］第三十七条　对被指示方行为的免责

a. 为执行申请人的指示，银行使用其他银行的服务，其费用和风险由申请人承担。

b. 即使银行主动选择了其他银行，如果发出指示未被执行，开证行或通知行对此亦不负责。

c. 当一家银行指示另一家银行提供服务时，指示银行有责任承担因执行相关指示而产生的任何佣金、手续费、成本费或其他开支（费用）。如果信用证规定上述费用由受益人承担，而该费用未能从信用证款项中收回或扣除，开证行依然承担支付此费用的责任。

信用证或其修改中不应规定通知受益人以通知行或第二通知行收到其费用为条件。

d. 申请人应受外国法律和惯例加诸银行的一切义务和责任的约束，并就此对银行承担补偿之责任。

［讲解］

开证人在办理开立信用证手续时，要填写开证申请书（application for opening Letter of Credit），将自己的要求，都填入申请书内。开证行根据申请书的内容，由自己或指示其他银行来执行。在执行过程中所产生的费用和风险，应该由申请人承担。如果开证行向另一家银行发出执行开证申请人的有关指示，但被通知行没有去履行，开证行也不承担责任。此外，当信用证规定有关费用由受益人承担，但实际上并未从证内应支付的款项中扣除时，开证行应负责支付该项费用。

[与第 500 号出版物比较]

本条与第 500 号出版物的第十八条内容基本相同。

[原文] Article 38 Transferable Credits

a. A bank is under no obligation to transfer a credit except to the extent and in the manner expressly consented to by that bank.

b. For the purpose of this article:

Transferable credit means a credit that specifically states it is "transferable". A transferable credit may be made available in whole or in part to another beneficiary ("second beneficiary") at the request of the beneficiary ("first beneficiary").

Transferring bank means a nominated bank that transfers the credit or, in a credit available with any bank, a bank that is specifically authorized by the issuing bank to transfer and that transfers the credit. An issuing bank may be a transferring bank.

Transferred credit means a credit that has been made available by the transferring bank to a second beneficiary.

c. Unless otherwise agreed at the time of transfer, all charges (such as commissions, fees, costs or expenses) incurred in respect of a transfer must be paid by the first beneficiary.

d. A credit may be transferred in part to more than one second beneficiary provided partial drawings or shipments are allowed.

A transferred credit cannot be transferred at the request of a second beneficiary to any subsequent beneficiary. The first beneficiary is not considered to be a subsequent beneficiary.

e. Any request for transfer must indicate if and under what conditions amendments may be advised to the second beneficiary. The transferred credit must clearly indicate those conditions.

f. If a credit is transferred to more than one second beneficiary, rejection of an amendment by one or more second beneficiary does not invalidate the acceptance by any other second beneficiary, with respect to which the transferred credit will be amended accordingly. For any second beneficiary that rejected the amendment, the transferred credit will remain unamended.

g. The transferred credit must accurately reflect the terms and conditions of the credit, including confirmation, if any, with the exception of:

- the amount of the credit,
- any unit price stated therein,
- the expiry date,
- the period for presentation, or
- the latest shipment date or given period for shipment,

any or all of which may be reduced or curtailed.

The percentage for which insurance cover must be effected may be increased to provide the amount of cover stipulated in the credit or these articles.

The name of the first beneficiary may be substituted for that of the applicant in the credit.

If the name of the applicant is specifically required by the credit to appear in any document other than the invoice, such requirement must be reflected in the transferred credit.

h. The first beneficiary has the right to substitute its own invoice and draft, if any, for those of a second beneficiary for an amount not in excess of that stipulated in the credit, and upon such substitution the first beneficiary can draw under the credit for the difference, if any, between its invoice and the invoice of a second beneficiary.

i. If the first beneficiary is to present its own invoice and draft, if any, but fails to do so on first demand, or if the invoices presented by the first beneficiary create discrepancies that did not exist in the presentation made by the second beneficiary and the first beneficiary fails to correct them on first demand, the transferring bank has the right to present the documents as received from the second beneficiary to the issuing bank, without further responsibility to the first beneficiary.

j. The first beneficiary may, in its request for transfer, indicate that honour or negotiation is to be effected to a second beneficiary at the place to which the credit has been transferred, up to and including the expiry date of the credit. This is without prejudice to the right of the first beneficiary in accordance with sub-article 38 (h).

k. Presentation of documents by or on behalf of a second beneficiary must be made to the transferring bank.

[译文] 第三十八条 可转让信用证

a. 除非银行明确同意其转让范围和转让方式，否则银行无义务办理转让信用证。

b. 就本条款而言：

可转让信用证意指明确表明“可转让”的信用证。根据受益人（第一受益人）的请求，可转让信用证可以全部或部分转让给其他受益人（第二受益人）。

转让银行意指转让信用证的指定银行。或者，在适用于任何银行的信用证中，转让银行是经开证行特别授权且办理信用证转让的银行。开证行也可成为转让银行。

转让信用证意指经转让银行办理转让后可供第二受益人使用的信用证。

c. 除非转让时另有约定，所有转让时产生的费用（诸如佣金、手续费、成本或开支）必须由第一受益人支付。

d. 只要信用证允许分批支款或分批装运，信用证可以分为若干部分转让给一个或以上的第二受益人。

第二受益人不得要求将信用证转让给居其后的其他受益人。第一受益人不属于上述其他受益人之列。

e. 任何有关转让的申请必须注明是否以及在何种条件下可以将信用证修改通知给第二受益人。可转让信用证必须明确注明上述条件。

f. 如果信用证转让给一个以上的第二受益人，其中一个或几个第二受益人拒绝接受信用证的修改，并不影响其他第二受益人对此信用证修改承兑的效力和接受相应修改。对于拒绝接受修改的第二受益人而言，该转让信用证即视为未被修改。

g. 可转让信用证必须准确表明原信用证的条款和条件，包括保兑（如有），但下列项目除外：

—信用证金额，

—规定的任何单价，

—到期日，

—单据提示期限，

—最迟装运日期或特定的装运期限。

以上任何一项或全部均可减少或缩短。

必须投保的保险金额比例可以增加，以满足原信用证或本惯例规定的保额。

可以用第一受益人的名称替换原信用证中申请人的名称。

如果原信用证特别要求开证申请人名称应在除发票以外的所有单据上出现时，则可转让信用证中必须表明该项要求。

h. 第一受益人有权用自己的发票和汇票（如有）来替换第二受益人的发票和汇票（如有），但其金额不得超过原信用证金额。在上述票据替换时，第一受益人可以在信用证下支取自己发票与第二受益人发票之间产生的差额（如有）。

i. 如果第一受益人要提交其自己的发票和汇票（如有），但却未能在首次被要求时据此办理。或者在第一受益人提交的发票中产生了不符点，且此不符点并非在第二受益人所提交发票中存在的，但是第一受益人未能在首次被要求时予以改正，则转让银行有权把从第二受益人收到的单据提交给开证行，并且不再对第一受益人负责。

j. 第一受益人可以在要求转让信用证时注明信用证受让地，并且在信用证的到期日之前（包括到期日）可以对第二受益人付款或议付。本条款并不损害第一受益人根据第三十八条（h）款拥有的权利。

k. 由第二受益人或代表第二受益人提交的单据必须提示给转让银行。

［讲解］

跟单信用证的含意是：银行应开证人的请求，开给受益人的一种用书面担保支付款项的承诺。只要受益人按照证内的规定去做——意即按规定时间，采用双方同意的运输方式，向对方发运约定数量和质量的货物，并且提供证内规定的各种合乎要求的单据。只要受益人提供的单据经银行审核正确无误，开证行就要保证支付款项。由此可见，信用证内的受益人，是证内规定各项内容的具体执行者，因而就要求受益人是固定的、不能随便更换。

但是，在国际贸易经营活动中，经常会出现信用证的受益人不一定是真正供货人的情况。例如，过去，我国对外贸易组织机构，基本采用原苏联的模式，即根据商品分类，组成几个大的专业总公司。如中国粮油食品进出口总公司、中国土产进出口总公司、中国杂品进出口总公司及中国五金矿产进出口总公司等。这些总公司与一些西方国家商人洽谈业务时，大多数采用跟单信用证方式。如中国土产进出口总公司与某国商人谈妥出口核桃仁一批，由于总公司本身没有货源，也不直接办理出口合同履行的一系列工作，于是便要求对方开来“不可撤销、可转让的跟单信用证”。待信用证开到后，总公司便将该证转让给天津土产进出口分公司，让其根据信用证内的要求执行供货任务。另外一种是现在常见的情况。例如一笔出口业务不是真正的供货商与国外用货商直接成交，而是通过中间商和用货商洽谈这笔业务的。国外用户找不到真正供货商，但与中间商熟悉，愿意和中间商达成交易并签订贸易合同。但由于中间商没有货物，并且往往还缺少资金。因而中间商就要另找供货商来完成交货任务，这就产生信用证的“转让”问题。所以，当交易达成后，中间商就在贸易合同中注明：买方（指国外客户）开来的信用证，应该是“不可撤销、可转让”的。如果国外客户同意，便开来以中间商为受益人、注明“可转让”的信用证。此证由中间商更改部分证内条款（如单价、装运期及有效期等）转让给供货商据以执行供货。供货商按证内规定发货后，获得货款。中间商则从原证与转让后的证内赚得差价（因为单价等条款变化）。此外，中间商也可能不更改原证条款而将信用证转让给供货商据以执行，由此获得供货商付给的佣金。

由于可转让信用证在形式、做法上与普通信用证有较大区别，所以惯例就专门为可转让信用证制定本条，以便于遵照执行。

1. 首先，信用证如果允许转让，证内必须明确规定该证是“可转让的”，如有“this credit is transferable”类似词句。可转让信用证允许将信用证内装运任务的全部或部分转让给第二受益人，允许它们全部/部分履行信用证内的交货任务。但信用证的“转让”，并非在第一受益人和第二受益人之间私下授受，而是要由银行办理信用证的转让工作。本条明确规定：转让银行是指办理信用证转让的被指定银行，或者，在适用于任何银行的信用证中，转让银行由开证行特别授权并办理转让信用证的银行。同时，开证行也可以担任转让行。由此可见，如果一份信用证规定该证可以转让时，是不允许受益人自行指定银行来办理转让工作的。

2. 转让信用证所产生的费用，由办理转让手续的一方承担。

通常这项工作是由原证的受益人，到证内指定银行办理转让工作的。所以，要向转让银行支付转让信用证的有关费用。

3. 如果原证规定货物可以分批支款或者分批装运，则可以分别转让给几个第二受益人。例如，一份可转让的出口 200 吨货物的信用证，证内规定允许分批装运。该证受益人自行出口 90 吨货物外，转让给青岛 H 公司执行出口 50 吨货物，转让给上海 P 公司执行出口 60 吨货物。这样做是可以的。但是，第二受益人不能再将所承担证内的发运货物数量再转让下去。如上所述，上海 P 公司如果只装出 40 吨货物后，就无力再发运货物，它不能将尚未装出 20 吨货物的装运任务，再转给其他单位来执行，但可将此 20 吨的装运任务退回给本证的转让人，这是允许的。

4. 原证的受益人（即第一受益人）在办理转让手续时，可以将原证照转，不更改证内的各项内容，只是另外规定第二受益人应执行交货的数量，或是信用证规定的全部/部分数量。另一种转让方式是将证内规定的各项条款作部分更动后再转让给第二受益人。证内可以更动的条款是有一定范围的。一般是下列几种：

(1) 货物的单价。转让后的单价，可比原证为低。第一受益人便可以赚取未转让前和转让后的两种单价之间的差价。

(2) 货物的金额。由于只转让部分数量或者由于单价有了变动，所以金额必然与原证金额不一致。

(3) 信用证有效期。为了防止第二受益人在履行交货任务时遇到意外情况，有必要留下一些时间来解决问题。所以，规定转让后信用证的有效期，往往要比原证要缩短一些。如原证的有效期为 7 月 31 日，转让后信用证的有效期可能提前 10 天或更多些。

(4) 交单日。为了上条所述的目的，转让后信用证内的交单期，也会短于原证规定的交单期。

(5) 装运期。为了上两条所述的目的，转让后信用证内的装运期，也会短于原证规定的装运期。

(6) 投保方面。如原证是在贸易术语CIF/CIP基础上开来的，则信用证转让时就会涉及保险方面的内容。第一受益人在办理信用证转让工作时，涉及险别和保险条款（CIC、ICC或AICC）方面的内容，是不能更改的。但在投保的加成上，是可以更动的，即不一定按原证投保加一成。如果第一受益人愿意，可以在转让后的信用证中，要求第二受益人按货值的120%甚至130%投保，转让人按惯例承诺支付超过按110%投保的保险费。这样做的目的是保障第一受益人的利益。因为第二受益人在交货过程中，货物一旦遭受损失时，第一受益人可以拿到超过货值110%的赔偿，然后将此笔赔款购买质较好、价格稍高的货物来完成原证规定的交货任务，以弥补原证开证人的损失。

(7) 关于原证的开证人。第一受益人为了不让第二受益人知道原开证人的名称，避免它们今后直接联系业务，影响到本身的经济利益。所以第一受益人在办理信用证的转让时，要求用自己的名称替换原证开证人的名称，这样做是可以的。

如果原证特别规定要求原开证人的名称应在除发票以外的任何单据中出现时，应该满足对方要求。即第二受益人提供的单据，应在除发票外，其他诸如提单、保险单、重量单及产地证等单据上都要有原开证人的名称。

第一受益人有权把由自己缮制出的发票和汇票，替换第二受益人制作的发票和汇票。这样，就把发票上的抬头人由第一受益人换为原开证人。因为转让信用证如果不是将原证不改动地转让，一般就会在单价等方面作改动后转让给第二受益人。后者缮制出的发票和汇票，必然由于单价等方面的变动而与原证不相符。在这种情况下，如果不更换发票和汇票，不仅造成“单证不符”，也泄露了第一受益人赚得差价的“天机”。至于其他单据，根据实际情况，可采取一些适当措施来满足原开证人的需要。

由于原证的其他条款，如品名、品质规格、贸易术语、运输方式等是不能更换的。有关装运地和目的地是否可以变更？需要根据成交使用的贸易术语和原证对这方面的规定来具体掌握。

5. 应该特别指出的是：原证的受益人在办理信用证转让手续时，必须明确说明该证以后的任何修改内容，是否也要无条件地通知第二受益人。同时，在几个第二受益人中，可以采取不同的态度来对待信用证修改的通知，一部分第二受益人表示同意接受修改，另一部分第二受益人可以表示拒绝接受修改。前者按修改后的要求执行信用证规定的任务，后者仍照原证规定办事，这样做是可以的。

在实际出口业务中，还有采用“背对背”信用证的做法。所谓“背对背”信用证，是指信用证的受益人本身不是货物的供应商，既无货物，也缺少资金，但有国外客户关系。他在与国外买方洽谈业务的同时，也与货物的供应商/生产商洽谈供应货物业务。该信用证的受益人目的就是以较低价购入的货物，转而以较高价格售予国外客户，从而赚取一买一卖之间的差额。具体的做法是：中间商收到国外进口商开来的信用证后，以此证为基础，转而申请另开一张信用证给供货商。这实际上是两份信用证。新开出的信用证除了受益人、开证人，单价、金额及装运/有效期等内容可与原证不同外，其他内容要与原证相同。用这种方法开出的信用证，称作“背对背”（back to back credit）。从做法上看，可转让信用证与背对背信用证似乎一致，但实际上，两种信用证是有很大区别的。表现如下。

（1）可转让信用证是原证内规定该证可以转让，在办理转让时，将信用证中的金额、数量等供货任务全部或部分转让给第二受益人，即货物供应商。信用证的转让，实际上是围绕一份信用证的转让活动。而背对背信用证却不同，它是原证没有注明该证可以转让，也就是不允许转让的情况下，该证的受益人打算转让该证，就不能用上述转让办法，只能采用“背对背”这种方式，来满足证内受益人供货给国外客户的任务，以及达到获取利润的目的。背对背信用证的开立，与第一份信用证的开证行及开证人没有关系。所以，原证与背对背信用证相比较，是相互独立的两份信用证。

(2) 可转让信用证是得到开证人及开证行的同意后开出的，证内注明有：本证允许转让字样。证内的第一受益人及转让后的第二受益人均居于同等地位，都可以得到原证开证行付款保证。而背对背信用证上的受益人，只可从本证的开证行处获得付款承诺，与原证的开证行和开证人无关。

目前，一些书刊杂志，甚至某些从事国际结算的机构都经常指出，背对背信用证内，一般都有以下的条款：“只有收到（第一份信用证的）开证行的付款时，本证的开证行才支付信用证项下的款项——大意”（payment of this L/C will be effected upon our receipt of funds from L/C opening bank and at our discretion, upon our negotiation of the documents）。如果证内有类似规定，实际上就使第二份信用证丧失它的独立作用，也就失去了信用证具有的特点——开证行根据单证相符原则就予以付款的承诺。这种规定，对第二受益人的风险是很大的，因为，第二份信用证的受益人对原证受益人的收款情况毫不知悉，如果原证受益人因为各种原因收不到货款时，第二受益人的货款便会落空。笔者认为：背对背信用证的开证人，为了推卸责任，往往在开出第二份信用证时，加上一些限制付款的条件如上面所述的条款，这是可以理解的。但不能认为，所有的背对背信用证，都一定会有限制付款的附加条件。再者，如果证内加注有附加条件，作为背对背信用证的受益人（供货人）是否能接受，也应该仔细考虑。供货人也可以要求开证人修改信用证，删除附加条件，作为履行合同的前提。

[与第500号出版物比较]

本条与第500号出版物中第四十八条内容类似。但在某些地方，还是有所区别。如本条对可转让信用证拟定了明确的定义，避免一些含义不清甚至错误的提法。再者，对转让费用由何方支付的问题，也做出明确规定。此外，本条还规定第一受益人可以保留不允许转让行将信用证的修改通知第二受益人的权利，借以保障第一受益人的利益。

［原文］Article 39　Assignment of Proceeds

The fact that a credit is not stated to be transferable shall not affect the right of the beneficiary to assign any proceeds to which it may be or may become entitled under the credit, in accordance with the provisions of applicable law. This article relates only to the assignment of proceeds and not to the assignment of the right to perform under the credit.

［译文］第三十九条　款项让渡

信用证未表明可转让，并不影响受益人根据所适用的法律规定，将其在该信用证项下有权获得的款项让渡与他人的权利。本条款所涉及的仅是款项的让渡，而不是信用证项下执行权力的让渡。

［讲解］

1．“款项让渡”，是指无论是何种类型的信用证，证内受益人都有权将从证内获得款项的权利，转让给其他人。这种提法，始见于本惯例 1974 年修订本第 290 号出版物的第四十七条，但内容很简单。自第 400 号出版物开始、继而第 500 号出版物及现在的第 600 号出版物内，都专设“款项让渡”条来规定这方面的内容。

2．在实际业务中，一般由于以下原因，造成信用证需要办理“款项让渡”手续。

（1）作为中间商的受益人，对外达成了出口业务后，但没有争取到国外客户同意开来可转让信用证，因而不能将原证全部或部分转让给供货人。如果供货人同意向国外买方先行供货，而货款则由中间商将证内的款项让渡给供货人，就可以采用“款项让渡”的办法，来解决中间商缺少偿付资金的问题。

（2）中间商没有争取到来证允许“可以转让”，而打算开出背对背信用证时，由于受自身条件（如资信等方面原因）的限制，银行不同意以原证为质押，向供货人开出背对背信用证。这时，只要得到供货人同意，中间商可以使用“货款让渡”的办法，来换取供货人按信用证规定的内容和要求，履行供货任务。应该明确的是，“款项让渡”涉及的仅是证内款项的转让，与原证开证人的利益没有冲突，也与开证人无关。而信用证的“转让”却不同，它涉及原证受益人执行信用证的权利。同时，在履行信用证的过程中，往往因受益人的更换，也会影响开证人的利益。所以，信用证需要转让时，一种做法是必须得到开证人同意，在开来的信用证内注有“允许转让”字样。另一种做法是受益人收到的信用证内，没有注明“允许转让”，受益人将该证交付银行作为质押，在开证人不知晓的情况下，向供货人另外开出一份新的信用证，这就是背对背信用证。此证就由供货人凭以履行供货任务。由此可见，信用证的“款项让渡”与信用证的“转让”，或者证内没有注明“允许转让”而开出背对背信用证，是完全不相同的。

3.“款项让渡”并非是当事人私下授受的行为，也需要办理相关手续，但各银行并无统一的做法。目前较普遍的做法是：当中间商，也就是款项让渡人，打算将证内款项转让给他人时，应到信用证内的指定银行办理“款项让渡”手续。什么是指定银行呢？例如来证是限定议付的，就到证内规定的议付银行办理。如来证是公开议付的，就到转让人准备办理单据押汇手续的银行办理。如果来证规定该证是不能议付的，则只能通过当地通知行代为向开证行办理等。

当办理“款项让渡”银行接受转让人的申请后，要给予书面确认。让渡人将银行的确认副本转交发货人——即“款项让渡”的受让人留存。将来发货人将货物装出后，向办理“款项转让”的银行提供信用证内规定的有关单据和货物已经装出的证明材料，银行则负责收款后直接将款项拨付发货人。

4. 从“款项让渡”的流程看，发货人只要持有银行接受办理“款项让渡”的确认，便可以放心将货装出。但实际上，“款项让渡”的做法对发货人隐藏着一些风险。

(1) 如果供货商按规定将货物装出，但中间商缮制出的结算单据不符合信用证的要求，造成单证不符，致使货款落空。发货人供货虽符合信用证要求，但同样也得不到款项。

(2) 当来证是“自由议付”的，中间商交单时，不将单据交给原发出同意办理“款项让渡”的银行，而交给另外一家银行办理交单收款手续。这样，中间商拿到了货款，但供货商却丧失了货款。

(3) 中间商有可能将信用证置之不顾，把货物售予另一家国外商人，自行收款。使发货人的货款回收无着，受到损失。

由此可见，虽然信用证惯例几次出版物专为“款项让渡”而设置一条规定，但银行并不保证供货人最后是否能够拿到款项。因此，供货人在表态是否同意接受这种付款方法之前，应该经过仔细考虑，特别要对中间商的资信情况要有所了解，避免上当受骗。

[与第 500 号出版物比较]

本条与第 500 号出版物的第四十九条的内容相同。

第二部分　简介《跟单信用证统一惯例》历次出版物主要内容

一、简介

自 19 世纪以来，随着国际贸易的发展，跟单信用证逐渐成为国际结算中的一种通用的支付方式。但是，由于国际上缺乏对跟单信用证有关当事人的权利、责任、条款的定义和术语的统一解释和公认标准，各国银行根据各自的习惯和利益各行其是。因此，信用证的各有关当事人之间的争议和纠纷经常发生。有的进口商和个别开证银行，往往过分挑剔单据上某一点不符要求，借此提出异议，拖延甚至拒绝支付款项。在这种情况下，国际商会为了减少因解释不同而引起的争端，调和各有关当事人之间的矛盾，经过反复开会讨论，制定并建议于 1930 年实行第一个有关信用证的惯例——《商业跟单信用证统一惯例》第 74 号出版物。该出版物实施时，使用的范围并不广泛，只得到两个经济贸易较发达国家即法国和比利时银行界的支持，而受到英、美等经济发达国家的抵制。虽然如此，承认并使用该惯例的各国银行界还是不断增多起来，待第一次修订公布实施《商业跟单信用证统一惯例（1933 年修订本）》第 82 号出版物时，使用该惯例的国家已经达到 40 个，但美国银行界直到 1938 年才在保留某些专对美国适用的特殊规定后，才采用此惯例。英国则是直到《商业跟单信用证统一惯例（1962 年修订本）》第 222 号出版物公布实行后，才采用此惯例。如今，世界各国、各地区银行界，基本上都采用此惯例。

二、《跟单信用证统一惯例》历次出版物的主要结构

（一）《商业跟单信用证统一惯例》（1929 年）第 74 号出版物

共分 5 类 46 条，其中：

A. 信用证的形式	9条
B. 义务	5条
C. 单据	18条
D. 条款解释	12条
E. 转让	2条

（二）《商业跟单信用证统一惯例（1933年修订本）》第82号出版物

共分5类49条，其中：

总则	
A. 信用证的形式	9条
B. 义务	5条
C. 单据	4条
提单	6条
铁路或内河运单、提货单存根	
邮包收据	3条
保险！	4条
发票	2条
其他单据	1条
D. 条款的解释	
“约”、“大约”或类似	
文字	1条
分批装运	2条
到期日和有效日	4条
装运、装船或发运	1条
交单	2条
展期	1条
日期条款	3条
E. 转让	1条

（三）《商业跟单信用证统一惯例（1951年修订本）》第151号出版物

共分5类49条，其中：

总则

A. 信用证的形式	8条
B. 义务	6条
C. 单据	4条
提单	6条
铁路提单等	3条
保险	4条
发票	2条
其他单据	1条
D. 条款解释	1条
分批装运	2条
到期日或有效期	4条
装运、装载或发运	1条
交单	2条
展期	1条
日期条款	3条
E. 转让	1条

（四）《商业跟单信用证统一惯例（1962年修订本）》第222号出版物

共分5类46条，其中：

总则和各项定义，分6点叙述

A. 信用证的形式和信用证的通知	6条
B. 义务和责任	6条
C. 单据	1条
证明装运或发货的单据（货运单据）	3条
海洋提单	5条

其他货运单据	2条
保险单据	6条
商业发票	1条
其他单据	1条
D. 其他规定	
数量和金额	1条
分批装运	2条
有效期和到期日	5条
装运、装船或发货	1条
交单	2条
日期名词	3条
E. 转让	1条

(五)《跟单信用证统一惯例(1974年修订本)》第290号出版物

共分5类47条，其中：

总则和定义，分6点叙述

A. 信用证的形式和通知	6条
B. 义务和责任	7条
C. 单据	1条
货运单据	4条
海洋提单	4条
联合运输单据	1条
其他货运单据	2条
保险单据	6条
商业发票	1条
其他单据	1条
D. 其他规定	
数量和金额	1条
分批装运	2条

有效期和到期日　　3条
装运、装船或发货　　1条
交单　　2条
日期名词　　3条
E. 转让　　2条

(六)《跟单信用证统一惯例（1983年修订本）》第400号出版物

共分5类49条，其中：

A. 总则和定义　　6条
B. 信用证的形式和通知　　8条
C. 义务和责任　　2条
C.1. 免责条款　　4条
C.2. 偿付　　1条
D. 单据　　3条
D.1. 运输单据（表明已装船或发运或接受监管的单据）　　10条
D.2. 保险单据　　6条
D.3. 商业发票　　1条
D.4 其他单据　　1条
E. 其他规定
数量与金额　　1条
分批支款及/或装运　　1条
分期支款及/或装运　　1条
日期和交单　　4条

(七)《跟单信用证统一惯例（1993年修订本）》第500号出版物

共分7类49条，其中：

A. 总则与定义　　5条
B. 信用证的形式与通知　　7条

C. 责任与义务	7 条
D. 单据	19 条
E. 杂项规定	9 条
F. 可转让信用证	1 条
G. 款项让渡	1 条

（八）《跟单信用证统一惯例（2007 年修订本）》第 600 号出版物

修订本的编排，不像过去按几大类区分，本次修订逐条叙述，共分 39 条。

第 1 条　统一惯例的适用范围
第 2 条　定义
第 3 条　释义
第 4 条　信用证与合同
第 5 条　单据与货物/服务/行为
第 6 条　适用性、有效期及提示地点
第 7 条　开证行的承诺
第 8 条　保兑行的承诺
第 9 条　关于信用证及修改的通知
第 10 条　信用证的修改
第 11 条　电讯传递与预先通知的信用证及其修改
第 12 条　指定
第 13 条　银行间偿付约定
第 14 条　审核单据的标准
第 15 条　相符提示
第 16 条　不符单据与不符点的通知
第 17 条　正本与副本单据
第 18 条　商业发票
第 19 条　至少包括两种不同运输方式的运输单据
第 20 条　提单

第21条　不可转让海运单
第22条　租船合约提单
第23条　空运单据
第24条　铁路或内陆水运单据
第25条　快递收据、邮政收据或投递证明
第26条　“货装舱面”、“托运人装载和计数”、“内容据托运人报称”及运费之外的费用
第27条　清洁运输单据
第28条　保险单据及保险范围
第29条　到期日或最迟交单日的延展
第30条　信用证金额、数量及单价的增减幅度
第31条　分批支款或分批装运
第32条　分期支款或分期装运
第33条　交单时间
第34条　单据有效性的免责
第35条　信息传递和翻译的免责
第36条　不可抗力
第37条　被指示方行为的免责
第38条　可转让信用证
第39条　款项让渡

附录一 Uniform Customs and Practice for Documentary Credits

— — — — — — — — — 1993 Revision — — — — — — — —

(ICC Publication No. 500)

A. GENERAL PROVISIONS AND DEFINITIONS

Article 1. Application of UCP

The Uniform Customs and Practice for Documentary Credits, 1993 Revision, ICC Publication No. 500, shall apply to all documentary Credits (including to the extent to which they may be applicable, Standby Letter (s) of Credit) where they are incorporated into the text of the Credit. They are binding on all parties thereto, unless otherwise expressly stipulated in the Credit.

Article 2. Meaning of Credit

For the purposes of these Articles, the expressions "Documentary Credit (s)" and "Standby Letter (s) of Credit" (hereinafter referred to as "Credit (s)"), mean any arrangement, however named or described, whereby a bank (the "Issuing Bank") acting at the request and on the instructions of a customer (the "Applicant") or on its own behalf,

i) is to make a payment to or to the order of a third party (the "Beneficiary"), or is to accept and pay bills of exchange (Draft (s)) drawn by the Beneficiary, or

ii) authorizes another bank to effect such payment, or to accept and pay such bills of exchange (Draft (s)), or

iii) authorizes another bank to negotiate, against stipulated document (s), provided that the terms and conditions of the Credit are complied with. For the purposes of these Articles, branches of a bank in different countries are considered another bank.

Article 3. Credits v. Contracts

a. Credits, by their nature, are separate transactions from the sales or other contract (s) on which they may be based and banks are in no way concerned with or bound by such contract (s), even if any reference whatsoever to such contract (s) is included in the Credit. Consequently, the undertaking of a bank to pay, accept and pay Draft (s) or negotiate and/or to fulfill any other obligation under the Credit, is not subject to claims or defences by the Applicant resulting from his relationships with the Issuing Bank or the Beneficiary.

b. A Beneficiary can in no case avail himself of the contractual relationships existing between the banks or between the Applicant and the Issuing Bank.

Article 4. Documents v. Goods/Services/Performances

In Credit operations all parties concerned deal with documents, and not with goods, services and/or other performances to which the documents may relate.

Article 5. Instructions to Issue/revise Credits

a. Instructions for the issuance of a Credit, the Credit itself, instructions for an amendment thereto, and the amendment itself, must be complete and precise. In order to guard against confusion and misunderstanding, banks should discourage any attempt.

i) to include excessive detail in the Credit or in any amendment thereto;

ii) to give instructions to issue, advise or confirm a Credit by reference to a Credit previously issued (similar Credit) where such previous Credit has been subject to accepted amendment (s), and/or unaccepted amendment (s),

b. All instructions for the issuance of a Credit and the Credit itself and, where applicable, all instructions for an amendment thereto and the amendment itself, must state precisely the document (s) against which payment, acceptance or negotiation is to be made.

B. FORM AND NOTIFICATIOIN OF CREDITS

Article 6. Revocable v. Irrevocable Credits

a. A Credit may be either

i) revocable, or

ii) irrevocable.

b. The Credit, therefore, should clearly indicate whether it is revocable or irrevocable.

c. In the absence of such indication the Credit shall be deemed to be irrevocable.

Article 7. Advising Bank's Liability

a. A Credit may be advised to a Beneficiary through another bank (the "Advising Bank") without engagement on the part of the Advising Bank, but that bank, if it elects to advise the Credit, shall take reasonable care to check the apparent authenticity of the Credit which it advises. If the bank elects not to advise the Credit, it must so inform the Issuing Bank without delay.

b. If the Advising Bank cannot establish such apparent authenticity it must inform, without delay, the bank from which the instructions appear to have been received that it has been unable to establish the authenticity of the Credit and if it elects nonetheless to advise the Credit it must inform the Beneficiary that it has not been able to establish the authenticity of the Credit.

Article 8. Revocation of a Credit

a. A revocable Credit may be amended or cancelled by the Issuing Bank at any moment and without prior notice to the Beneficiary.

b. However, the Issuing Bank must:

i) reimburse another bank with which a revocable Credit has been made available for sight payment, acceptance or negotiation—for any payment, acceptance or negotiation made by such bank—prior to receipt by it of notice of amendment or cancellation, against documents which appear on their face to be in compliance with the terms and conditions of the Credit,

ii) reimburse another bank with which a revocable Credit has been made available for deferred payment, if such a bank has, prior to receipt by it of notice of amendment or cancellation, taken up documents which appear on their face to be in compliance with the terms and conditions of the Credit.

Article 9. Liability of Issuing and Confirming Banks

a. An irrevocable Credit constitutes a definite undertaking of the Issuing Bank, provided that the stipulated documents are presented to the Nominated Bank or to the Issuing Bank and that the terms and conditions of the Credit are complied with:

i) if the Credit provides for sight payment—to pay at sight;

ii) if the Credit provides for deferred payment—to pay on the maturity date (s) determinable in accordance with the stipulations of the Credit;

iii) if the Credit provides for acceptance;

(a) by the Issuing Bank—to accept Draft (s) drawn by the Beneficiary on the Issuing Bank and pay them at maturity, or

(b) by another drawee bank—to accept and pay at maturity Draft (s) drawn by the Beneficiary on the Issuing Bank in the event the drawee bank stipulated in the Credit does not accept Draft (s) drawn on it, or to pay Draft (s) accepted but not paid by such drawee bank at maturity;

iv) if the Credit provides for negotiation—to pay without recourse to drawers and/or bona-fide holders, Draft (s) drawn by the Beneficiary and/or document (s) presented under the Credit. A Credit should not be issued available by Draft (s) on the Applicant. If the Credit nevertheless calls for Draft (s) on the Applicant, banks will consider such Draft (s) as an additional document (s).

b. A confirmation of an irrevocable Credit by another bank (the "Confirming Bank") upon the authorization or request of the Issuing Bank, constitutes a definite undertaking of the Confirming Bank, in addition to that of the Issuing Bank, provided that the stipulated documents are presented to the Confirming Bank or to any other Nominated Bank and that the terms and conditions of the Credit are complied with:

i) if the Credit provides for sight payment—to pay at sight;

ii) if the Credit provides for deferred payment—to pay on the maturity date (s) determinable in accordance with the stipulations of the Credit;

iii) if the Credit provides for acceptance:

(a) by the Confirming Bank—to accept Draft (s) drawn by the Beneficiary on the Confirming Bank and pay them at maturity, or

(b) by another drawee bank—to accept and pay at maturity Draft (s) drawn by the Beneficiary on the Confirming Bank, in the event the drawee bank stipulated in the Credit does not accept Draft (s) drawn on it, or to pay Draft (s) accepted but not paid by such drawee bank at maturity;

iv) if the Credit provides for negotiation to negotiate without recourse to drawers and/or bona fide holders, Draft (s) drawn by the Beneficiary and/or document (s) presented under the Credit. A Credit should not be issued available by Draft (s) on the Applicant. If the Credit nevertheless calls for Draft (s) on the Applicant, banks will consider such Draft (s) as an additional document (s).

c. i) If another bank is authorized or requested by the Issuing Bank to add its confirmation to a Credit but is not prepared to do so, it must so inform the Issuing Bank without delay.

ii) Unless the Issuing Bank specifies otherwise in its authorization or request to add confirmation, the Advising Bank may advise the Credit to the Beneficiary without adding its confirmation.

d. i) Except as otherwise provided by Article 48, an Irrevocable Credit can neither be amended nor cancelled without the agreement of the Issuing Bank, the Confirming Bank, if any, and the Beneficiary.

ii) The Issuing Bank shall be irrevocably bound by an amendment (s) issued by it from the time of the issuance of such amendment (s). A Confirming Bank may extend its confirmation to an amendment and shall be irrevocably bound as of the time of its advice of the amendment. A Confirming Bank may, however, choose to advise an amendment to the Beneficiary without extending its confirmation and if so, must inform the Issuing Bank and the Beneficiary without delay.

iii) The terms of the original Credit (or a Credit incorporating previously accepted amendment (s)) will remain in force for the Beneficiary until the Beneficiary communicates his acceptance of the amendment to the bank that advised such amendment. The Beneficiary should give notification of acceptance or rejection of amendment (s). If the Beneficiary fails to give such notification, the tender of documents to the Nominated Bank or Issuing Bank, that conform to the Credit and to not yet accepted amendment (s), will be deemed to be notification of acceptance by the Beneficiary of such amendment (s) and as of that moment the Credit will be amended.

iv) Partial acceptance of amendments contained in one and the same advice of amendment is not allowed and consequently will not be give any effect.

Article 10. Types of Credit

a. All Credits must clearly indicate whether they are available by sight payment, by deferred payment, by acceptance or by negotiation.

b. i) Unless the Credit stipulates that it is available only with the Issuing Bank, all Credits must nominate the bank (the "Nominated Bank") which is authorized to pay, to incur a deferred payment undertaking, to accept Draft (s) or to negotiate. In a freely negotiable Credit, any bank is a Nominated Bank Presentation of documents must be made to the Issuing Bank or the Confirming Bank, if any, or any other Nominated Bank. Negotiation means the giving of value for Draft (s) and/or document (s) by the bank authorized to negotiate. Mere examination of the documents without giving of value does not constitute a negotiation.

c. Unless the Nominated Bank is the Confirming Bank, nomination by the Issuing Bank does not constitute any undertaking by the Nominated Bank to pay, to incur a deferred payment undertaking, to accept Draft (s), or to negotiate. Except where expressly agreed to by the Nominated Bank and so communicated to the Beneficiary, the Nominated Bank's receipt of and/or examination and/or forwarding of the documents does not make that bank liable to pay, to incur a deferred payment undertaking, to accept Draft (s), or to negotiate.

d. By nominating another bank, or by allowing for negotiation by any bank, or by authorizing or requesting another bank to add its confirmation, the Issuing Bank authorizes such bank to pay, accept Draft (s) or negotiate as the case may be, against documents which appear on their face to be in compliance with the terms and conditions of the Credit and undertakes to reimburse such bank in accordance with the provisions of these Articles.

Article 11. Teletransmitted and Pre-Advised Credits

a. i) When an Issuing Bank instructs an Advising Bank by an authenticated teletransmission to advise a Credit or an amendment to a Credit, the teletransmission will be deemed to be the operative Credit instrument or the operative amendment, and no mail confirmation should be sent. Should a mail confirmation nevertheless be sent, it will have no effect and the Advising Bank will have no obligation to check such mail confirmation against the operative Credit instrument or the operative amendment received by teletransmission.

ii) If the teletransmission states "full details to follow" (or words of similar effect) or states that the mail confirmation is to be the operative Credit instrument or the operative amendment, then the teletransmission will not be deemed to be the operative Credit instrument or the operative amendment. The Issuing Bank must forward the operative Credit instrument or the operative amendment to such Advising Bank without delay.

b. If a bank uses the services of an Advising Bank to have the Credit advised to the Beneficiary, it must also use the services of the same bank for advising an amendment (s).

c. A preliminary advice of the issuance or amendment of an irrevocable Credit (pre-advice), shall only be given by an Issuing Bank if such bank is prepared to issue-the operative Credit instrument or the operative amendment thereto. Unless otherwise stated in such preliminary advice by the Issuing Bank, an Issuing Bank having given such pre-advice shall be irrevocably committed to issue or amend the Credit, in terms not inconsistent with the pre-advice, without delay.

Article 12. Incomplete or Unclear Instructions

If incomplete or unclear instructions are received to advise, confirm or amend a Credit, the bank requested to act on such instructions may give preliminary notification to the Beneficiary for information only and without responsibility. This preliminary notification should state clearly that the notification is provided for information only and without the responsibility of the Advising Bank. In any event, the Advising Bank must inform the Issuing Bank of the action taken and request it to provide the necessary information.

The Issuing Bank must provide the necessary information without delay. The Credit will be advised, confirmed or amended, only when complete and clear instructions have been received and if the Advising Bank is then prepared to act on the instructions.

C. LIABILITIES AND RESPONSIBILITIES

Article 13. Standard for Examination of Documents

a. Banks must examine all documents stipulated in the Credit with reasonable care, to ascertain whether or not they appear, on their face, to be in compliance with the terms and conditions of the Credit. Compliance of the stipulated documents on their face with the terms and conditions of the Credit, shall be determined by international standard banking practice as reflected in these Articles. Documents which appear on their face to be inconsistent with one another will be considered as not appearing on their face to be in compliance with the terms and conditions of the Credit. Documents not stipulated in the Credit will not be examined by banks. If they receive such documents, they shall return them to the presenter or pass them on without responsibility.

b. The Issuing Bank, the Confirming Bank, if any, or a Nominated Bank acting on their behalf, shall each have a reasonable time, not to exceed seven banking days following the day of receipt of the documents, to examine the documents and determine whether to take up or refuse the documents and to inform the party from which it received the documents accordingly.

c. If a Credit contains conditions without stating the document (s) to be presented in compliance therewith, banks will deem such conditions as not stated and will disregard them.

Article 14. Discrepant Documents and Notice

a. When the Issuing Bank authorizes another bank to pay, incur a deferred payment undertaking, accept Draft (s), or negotiate against documents which appear on their face to be in compliance with the terms and conditions of the Credit, the Issuing Bank and the Confirming Bank, if any, are bound:

i) to reimburse the Nominated Bank which has paid, incurred a deferred payment undertaking, accepted Draft (s), or negotiated,

ii) to take up the documents.

b. Upon receipt of the documents the Issuing Bank and/or Confirming Bank, if any, or a Nominated Bank acting on their behalf, must determine on the basis of the documents alone whether or not they appear on their face to be in compliance with the terms and conditions of the Credit. If the documents appear on their face not to be in compliance with the terms and conditions of the Credit, such banks may refuse to take up the documents.

c. If the Issuing Bank determines that the documents appear on their face not to be in compliance with the terms and conditions of the Credit, it may in its sole judgment approach the Applicant for a waiver of the discrepancy (ies). This does not, however, extend the period mentioned in sub-Article 13 (b).

d. i) If the Issuing Bank and/or Confirming Bank, if any, or a Nominated Bank acting on their behalf, decides to refuse the documents, it must give notice to that effect by telecommunication or, if that is not possible, by other expeditious means, without delay but no later than the close of the seventh banking day following the day of receipt of the documents. Such notice shall be given to the bank from which it received the documents, or to the Beneficiary, if it received the documents directly from him.

ii) Such notice must state all discrepancies in respect of which the bank refuses the documents and must also state whether it is holding the documents at the disposal of, or is returning them to, the presenter.

iii) The Issuing Bank and/or Confirming Bank, if any, shall then be entitled to claim from the remitting bank refund, with interest, of any reimbursement which has been made to that bank.

e. If the Issuing Bank and/or Confirming Bank, if any, fails to act in accordance with the provisions of this Article and/or fails to hold the documents at the disposal of, or return them to the presenter, the Issuing Bank and/or Confirming Bank, if any, shall be precluded from claiming that the documents are not in compliance with the terms and conditions of the Credit.

f. If the remitting bank draws the attention of the Issuing and/or Confirming Bank, if any, to any discrepancy (ies) in the document (s) or advises such banks that it has paid, incurred a deferred payment undertaking, accepted Draft (s) or negotiated under reserve or against an indemnity in respect of such discrepancy (ies), the Issuing Bank and/or Confirming Bank, if any, shall not be thereby relieved from any of their obligations under any provision of this Article. Such reserve or indemnity concerns only the relations between the remitting bank and the party towards whom the reserve was made, or from whom, or on whose behalf, the indemnity was obtained.

Article 15. Disclaimer on Effectiveness of Documents

Banks assume no liability or responsibility for the form, sufficiency, accuracy, genuineness, falsification or legal effect of any document (s), or for the general and/or particular conditions stipulated in the document (s) or superimposed thereon; nor do they assume any liability or responsibility for the description, quantity, weight, quality, condition, packing, delivery, value or existence of the goods represented by any document (s), or for the good faith or acts and/or omissions, solvency, performance or standing of the consignors, the carriers, the forwarders, the consignees or the insurers of the goods, or any other person whomsoever.

Article 16. Disclaimer on the Transmission of Messages

Banks assume no liability or responsibility for the consequences arising out of delay and/or loss in transit of any message (s), letter (s) or document (s), or for delay, mutilation or other error (s) arising in the transmission of any telecommunication. Banks assume no liability or responsibility for errors in translation and/or interpretation of technical terms, and reserve the right to transmit Credit terms without translating them.

Article 17. Force Majeure

Banks assume no liability or responsibility for the consequences arising out of the interruption of their business by Acts of God, riots, civil commotions, insurrections, wars or any other causes beyond their control, or by any strikes or lockouts. Unless specifically authorized, banks will not, upon resumption of their business, pay, incur a deferred payment undertaking, accept Draft (s) or negotiate under Credits which expired during such interruption of their business.

Article 18. Disclaimer for Acts of an Instructed Party

a. Banks utilizing the services of another bank or other banks for the purpose of giving effect to the instructions of the Applicant do so for the account and at the risk of such Applicant.

b. Banks assume no liability or responsibility should the instructions they transmit not be carried out, even if they have themselves taken the initiative in the choice of such other bank (s),

c. i) A party instructing another party to perform services is liable for any charges, including commissions, fees, costs or expenses incurred by the instructed party in connections with its instructions.

ii) Where a Credit stipulates that such charges are for the account of a party other than the instructing party, and charges cannot be collected, the instructing party remains ultimately liable for the payment thereof.

d. The Applicant shall be bound by and liable to indemnify the banks against all obligations and responsibilities imposed by foreign laws and usages.

Article 19. Bank-to-Bank Reimbursement Arrangements

a. If an Issuing Bank intends that the reimbursement to which a paying, accepting or negotiating bank is entitled, shall be obtained by such bank (the "Claiming Bank"), claiming on another party (the "Reimbursing Bank"), it shall provide such Reimbursing Bank in good time with the proper instructions or authorization to honour such reimbursement claims.

b. Issuing Banks shall not require a Claiming Bank to supply a certificate of compliance with the terms and conditions of the Credit to the Reimbursing Bank.

c. An Issuing Bank shall not be relieved from any of its obligations to provide reimbursement if and when reimbursement is not received by the Claiming Bank from the Reimbursing Bank.

d. The Issuing Bank shall be responsible to the Claiming Bank for any loss of interest if reimbursement is not provided by the Reimbursing Bank on first demand, or as otherwise specified in the Credit, or mutually agreed, as the case may be.

e. The reimbursing Bank's charges should be for the account of the Issuing Bank. However, in cases where the charges are for the account of another party, it is the responsibility of the Issuing Banks to so indicate in the original Credit and in the reimbursement authorization. In cases where the Reimbursing Bank's charges are for the account of another party they shall be collected from the Claiming Bank when the Credit is drawn under. In cases where the Credit is not drawn under, the Reimbursing Bank's charges remain the obligation of the Issuing Bank.

D. DOCUMENTS

Article 20. Ambiguity as to the Issuers of Documents

a. Terms such as "first class", "well known", "qualified", "independent", "official", "competent", "local" and the like, shall not be used to describe the issuers of any document (s) to be presented under a Credit. If such terms are incorporated in the Credit, banks will accept the relative document (s) as presented, provided that it appears on its face to be in compliance with the other terms and conditions of the Credit and not to have been issued by the Beneficiary.

b. Unless otherwise stipulated in the Credit, banks will also accept as an original document (s), a document (s) produced or appearing to have been produced:

i) by reprographic, automated or computerized systems;

ii) as carbon copies;

provided that it is marked as original and, where necessary, appears to be signed. A document may be signed by handwriting, by facsimile signature, by perforated signature, by stamp, by symbol, or by any other mechanical or electronic method of authentication.

c. i) Unless otherwise stipulated in the Credit, banks will accept as a copy (ies), a document (s) either labelled copy or not marked as an original—a copy (ies) need not be signed.

ii) Credits that require multiple document (s) such as "duplicate", "two fold", "two copies" and the like, will be satisfied by the presentation of one original and the remaining number in copies except where the document itself indicates otherwise.

d. Unless otherwise stipulated in the Credit, a condition under a Credit calling for a document to be authenticated, validated, legalized, visaed, certified or indicating a similar requirement, will be satisfied by any signature, mark, stamp or label on such document that on its face appears to satisfy the above condition.

Article 21. Unspecified Issuers or Contents of Documents

When documents other than transport documents, insurance documents and commercial invoices are called for, the Credit should stipulate by whom such documents are to be issued and their wording or data content. If the Credit does not so stipulate, banks will accept such documents as presented, provided that their data content is not inconsistent with any other stipulated document presented.

Article 22. Issuance Date of Documents v. Credit Date

Unless otherwise stipulated in the Credit, banks will accept a document bearing a date of issuance prior to that of the Credit, subject to such document being presented within the time limits set out in the Credit and in these Articles.

Article 23. Marine/Ocean Bill of Lading

a. If a Credit calls for a bill of lading covering a port-to-port shipment, banks will, unless otherwise stipulated in the Credit, accept a document, however named, which:

i) appears on its face to indicate the name of the carrier and to have been signed or otherwise authenticated by:

– the carrier or a named agent for or on behalf of the carrier, or

– the master or a named agent for or on behalf of the master.

Any signature or authentication of the carrier or master must be identified as carrier or master, as the case may be. An agent signing or authenticating for the carrier or master must also indicate the name and the capacity of the party, i. e. carrier or master, on whose behalf that agent is acting, and

ii) indicates that the goods have been loaded on board, or shipped on a named vessel. Loading on board or shipment on a named vessel may be indicated by pre-printed wording on the bill of lading that the goods have been loaded on board a named vessel or shipped on a named vessel, in which case the date of issuance of the bill of lading will be deemed to be the date of loading on board and the date of shipment. In all other cases loading on board a named vessel must be evidenced by a notation on the bill of lading which gives the date on which the goods have been loaded on board, in which case the date of the on board notation will be deemed to be the date of shipment. If the bill of lading contains the indication "intended vessel", or similar qualification in relation to the vessel, loading on board a named vessel must be evidenced by an on board notation on the bill of lading which, in addition to the date on which the goods have been loaded on board, also includes the name of the vessel on which the goods have been loaded, even if they have been loaded on the vessel named as the "intended vessel". If the bill of lading indicates a place of receipt or taking in charge different from the port of loading, the on board notation must also include the port of loading stipulated in the Credit and the name of the vessel on which the goods have been loaded, even if they have been loaded on the vessel named in the bill of lading. This provision also applies whenever loading on board the vessel is indicated by pre-printed wording on the bill of lading, and

iii) indicates the port of loading and the port of discharge stipulated in the credit, notwithstanding that it:

(a) indicates a place of taking in charge different from the port of loading, and/or a place of final destination different from the port of discharge, and/or

(b) contains the indication "intended" or similar qualification in relation to the port of loading and/or port of discharge, as long as the document also states the ports of loading and/or discharge stipulated in the Credit, and

iv) consists of a sole original bill of lading, or if issued in more than one original, the full set as so issued, and

v) appears to contain all of the terms and conditions of carriage, or some of such terms and conditions by reference to a source or document other than the bill of lading (short form/blank back bill of lading), banks will not examine the contents of such terms and conditions, and

vi) contains no indication that it is subject to a charter party and/or no indication that the carrying vessel is propelled by sail only, and

vii) in all other respects meets the stipulations of the Credit.

b. For the purpose of this Article, transhipment means unloading and reloading from one vessel to another vessel during the course of ocean carriage from the port of loading to the port of discharge stipulated in the Credit.

c. Unless transhipment is prohibited by the terms of the Credit, banks will accept a bill of lading which indicates that the goods will be transhipped, provided that the entire ocean carriage is covered by one and the same bill of lading.

d. Even if the Credit prohibits transhipment, banks will accept a bill of lading which:

i) indicates that transhipment will take place as long as the relevant cargo is shipped in Container (s), Trailer (s) and/or "LASH" barge (s) as evidenced by the bill of lading, provided that the entire ocean carriage is covered by one and the same bill of lading, and/or

ii) incorporates clauses stating that the carrier reserves the right to tranship.

Article 24. Non-Negotiable Sea Waybill

a. If a Credit calls for a non-negotiable sea waybill covering a port-to-port shipment, banks will, unless otherwise stipulated in the Credit, accept a document, however named, which:

i) appears on its face to indicate the name of the carrier and to have been signed or otherwise authenticated by:

– the carrier or a named agent for or on behalf of the carrier, or

– the master or a named agent for or on behalf of the master.

Any signature or authentication of the carrier or master must be identified as carrier or master, as the case may be. An agent signing or authenticating for the carrier or master must also indicate the name and the capacity of the party, i. e. carrier or master, on whose behalf that agent is acting, and

ii) indicates that the goods have been loaded on board, or shipped on a named vessel. Loading on board or shipment on a named vessel may be indicated by pre-printed wording on the non-negotiable sea waybill that the goods have been loaded on board a named vessel or shipped on a named vessel, in which case the date of issuance of the non-negotiable sea waybill will be deemed to be the date of loading on board and the date of shipment. In all other cases loading on board a named vessel must be evidenced by a notation on the non-negotiable sea way bill which gives the date on which the goods have been loaded on board, in which case the date of the on board notation will be deemed to be the date of shipment. If the non-negotiable sea waybill contains the indication "intended vessel", or similar qualification in relation to the vessel, loading on board a named vessel must be evidenced by an on board notation on the non-negotiable sea waybill which, in addition to the date on which the goods have been loaded on board, includes the name of the vessel on which the goods have been loaded, even if they have been loaded on the vessel named as the "intended vessel". If the non-negotiable sea waybill indicates a place of receipt or taking in charge different from the port of loading, the on board notation must also include the port of loading stipulated in the Credit and the name of the vessel on which the goods have been loaded, even if they have been loaded on a vessel named in the on-negotiable sea waybill. This provision also applies whenever loading on board the vessel is indicated by pre-printed wording on the non – negotiable sea waybill, and

iii) indicates the port of loading and the port of discharge stipulated in the Credit, notwithstanding that it:

(a) indicates a place of taking in charge different from the port of loading, and/or a place of final destination different from the port discharge, and/or

(b) contains the indication "intended" or similar qualification in relation to the port of loading and/or port of discharge, as long as the document also states the ports of loading and/or ports of discharge stipulated in the Credit, and

iv) consists of a sole original non-negotiable sea waybill, or if issued in more than one original, the full set as so issued, and

v) appears to contain all of the terms and conditions of carriage, or some of such terms and conditions by reference to a source or document other than the non-negotiable sea waybill (short form/blank back non-negotiable sea waybill); banks will not examine the contents of such terms and conditions, and

vi) contains no indication that it is subject to a charter party and/or no indication that the carrying vessel is propelled by sail only, and

vii) in all other respects meets the stipulations of the Credit.

b. For the purpose of this Article, transhipment means unloading and reloading from one vessel to another vessel during the course of ocean carriage from the port of loading to the port of discharge stipulated in the Credit.

c. Unless transhipment is prohibited by the terms of the Credit, banks will accept a non-negotiable sea waybill which indicates that the goods will be transhipped, provided that the entire ocean carriage is covered by one and the same non-negotiable sea waybill.

d. Even if the Credit prohibits transhipment, banks will accept a non-negotiable sea waybill which:

i) indicates that transhipment will take place as long as the relevant cargo is shipped in Container (s), Trailer (s) and/or "LASH" barge (s) as evidenced by the non-negotiable sea waybill, provided that the entire ocean carriage is covered by one and the same non-negotiable sea waybill, and/or

ii) incorporates clauses stating that the carrier reserves the right to tranship.

Article 25. Charter Party Bill of Lading

a. If a Credit calls for or permits a charter party bill of lading, banks will, unless otherwise stipulated in the Credit, accept a document, however named, which:

i) contains any indication that it is subject to a charter party, and

ii) appears on its face to have been signed or otherwise authenticated by:

– the master or a named agent for or on behalf of the master, or

– the owner or a named agent for or on behalf of the owner.

Any signature or authentication of the master or owner must be identified as master or owner as the case may be. An agent signing or authenticating for the master or owner must also indicate the name and the capacity of the party, i. e. master or owner, on whose behalf that agent is acting, and

iii) does or does not indicate the name of the carrier, and

iv) indicates that the goods have been loaded on board or shipped on a named vessel. Loading on board or shipment on a named vessel may be indicated by pre-printed wording on the bill of lading that the goods have been loaded on board a named vessel or shipped on a named vessel, in which case the date of issuance of the bill of lading will be deemed to be the date of loading on board and the date of shipment.

In all other cases loading on board a named vessel must be evidenced by a notation on the bill of lading which gives the date on which the goods have been loaded on board, in which case the date of the on board notation will be deemed to be the date of shipment, and

v) indicates the port of loading and the port of discharge stipulated in the Credit, and

vi) consists of a sole original bill of lading or, if issued in more than one original, the full set as so issued, and

vii) contains no indication that the carrying vessel is propelled by sail only, and

viii) in all other respects meets the stipulations of the Credit.

b. Even if the Credit requires the presentation of a charter party contract in connection with a charter party bill of lading, banks will not examine such charter party contract, but will pass it on without responsibility on their part.

Article 26. Multimodal Transport Document

a. If a Credit calls for a transport document covering at least two different modes of transport (multimodal transport), banks will, unless otherwise stipulated in the Credit, accept a document, however named, which:

i) appears on its face to indicate the name of the carrier or multimodal transport operator and to have been signed or otherwise authenticated by:

– the carrier or multimodal transport operator or a named agent for or on behalf of the carrier or multimodal transport operator,

– the master or a named agent for or on behalf of the master.

Any signature or authentication of the carrier, multimodal transport operator or master must be identified as carrier, multimodal transport operator or master, as the case may be. An agent signing or authenticating for the carrier, multimodal transport operator or master must also indicate the name and the capacity of the party, i. e. carrier, multimodal transport operator or master, on whose behalf that agent is acting, and

ii) indicates that the goods have been dispatched, taken in charge or loaded on board. Dispatch, taking in charge or loading on board may be indicated by wording to that effect on the multimodal transport document and the date of issuance will be deemed to be the date of dispatch, taking in charge or loading on board and the date of shipment. However, if the document indicates, by stamp or otherwise, a date of dispatch, taking in charge or loading on board, such date will be deemed to be the date of shipment, and

iii) (a) indicates the place of taking in charge stipulated in the Credit which may be different from the port, airport or place of loading, and the place of final destination stipulated in the Credit which may be different from the port, airport or place of discharge, and/or

(b) contains the indication "intended" or similar qualification in relation to the vessel and/or port of loading and/or port of discharge, and

iv) consists of a sole original multimodal transport document or, if issued in more than one original, the full set as so issued, and

v) appears to contain all of the terms and conditions of carriage, or some of such terms and conditions by reference to a source or document other than the multimodal transport document (short form/blank back multimodal transport document); banks will not examine the contents of such terms and conditions, and

vi) contains no indication that it is subject to a charter party and/or no indication that the carrying vessel is propelled by sail only, and

vii) in all other respects meets the stipulations of the Credit.

b. Even if the Credit prohibits transhipment, banks will accept a multimodal transport document which indicates that transhipment will or may take place, provided that the entire carriage is covered by one and the same multimodal transport document.

Article 27. Air Transport Document

a. If a Credit calls for an air transport document, banks will, unless otherwise stipulated in the Credit, accept a document, however named, which:

i) appears on its face to indicate the name of the carrier and to have been signed or otherwise authenticated by:

- the carrier, or
- a named agent for or on behalf of the carrier;

Any signature or authentication of the carrier must be identified as carrier. An agent signing or authenticating for the carrier must also indicate the name and the capacity of the party, i. e. carrier, on whose behalf that agent is acting, and

ii) indicates that the goods have been accepted for carriage, and

iii) where the Credit calls for an actual date of dispatch, indicates a specific notation of such date, the date of dispatch so indicated on the air transport document will be deemed to be the date of shipment.

For the purpose of this Article, the information appearing in the box on the air transport document (marked "For Carrier Use Only" or similar expression) relative to the flight number and date will not be considered as a specific notation of such date of dispatch. In all other cases, the date of issuance of the air transport document will be deemed to be the date of shipment, and

iv) indicates the airport of departure and the airport of destination stipulated in the Credit, and

v) appears to be the original for consignor/shipper even if the Credit stipulates a full set of originals, or similar expressions, and

vi) appears to contain all of the terms and conditions of carriage, or some of such terms and conditions, by reference to a source or document other than the air transport document; banks will not examine the contents of such terms and conditions, and

vii) in all other respects meet the stipulations of the Credit.

b. For the purpose of this Article, transhipment means unloading and reloading from one aircraft to another aircraft during the course of carriage from the airport of departure to the airport of destination stipulated in the Credit.

c. Even if the Credit prohibits transhipment, banks will accept an air transport document which indicates that transhipment will or may take place, provided that the entire carriage is covered by one and the same air transport document.

Article 28. Road, Rail or Inland Waterway Transport Documents

a. If a Credit calls for a road, rail, or inland waterway transport document, banks will, unless otherwise stipulated in the Credit, accept a document of the type called for, however named, which:

i) appears on its face to indicate the name of the carrier and to have been signed or otherwise authenticated by the carrier or a named agent for or on behalf of the carrier and/or to bear a reception stamp or other indication of receipt by the carrier or a named agent for or on behalf of the carrier.

Any signature, authentication, reception stamp or other indication of receipt of the carrier, must be identified on its face as that of the carrier.

An agent signing or authenticating for the carrier, must also indicate the name and the capacity of the party, i. e. carrier, on whose behalf that agent is acting, and

ii) indicates that the goods have been received for shipment, dispatch or carriage or wording to this effect. The date of issuance will be deemed to be the date of shipment unless the transport document contains a reception stamp, in which case the date of the reception stamp will be deemed to be the date of shipment, and

iii) indicates the place of shipment and the place of destination stipulated in the Credit, and

iv) in all other respects meet the stipulations of the Credit.

b. In the absence of any indication on the transport document as to the numbers issued, banks will accept the transport document (s) presented as constituting a full set. Banks will accept as original (s) the transport document (s) whether marked as original (s) or not.

c. For the purpose of this Article, transhipment means unloading and reloading from one means of conveyance to another means of conveyance, in different modes of transport, during the course of carriage from the place of shipment to the place of destination stipulated in the Credit.

d. Even if the Credit prohibits transhipment, banks will accept a road, rail, or inland waterway transport document which indicates that transhipment will or may take place, provided that the entire carriage is covered by one and the same transport document and within the same mode of transport.

Article 29. Courier and Post Receipts

a. If a Credit calls for a post receipt or certificate of posting, banks will, unless otherwise stipulated in the Credit, accept a post receipt or certificate of posting which:

i) appears on its face to have been stamped or otherwise authenticated and dated in the place from which the Credit stipulates the goods are to be shipped or dispatched and such date will be deemed to be the date of shipment or dispatch, and

ii) in all other respects meet the stipulations of the Credit.

b. If a Credit calls for a document issued by a courier or expedited delivery service evidencing receipt of the goods for delivery, banks will, unless otherwise stipulated in the Credit, accept a document, however named, which:

i) appears on its face to indicate the name of the courier/service, and to have been stamped, signed or otherwise authenticated by such named courier/service (unless the Credit specifically calls for a document issued by a named Courier/Service, banks will accept a document issued by any Courier/Service), and

ii) indicates a date of pick-up or of receipt or wording to this effect, such date being deemed to be the date of shipment or dispatch, and

iii) in all other respects meet the stipulations of the Credit.

Article 30. Transport Documents issued by Freight Forwarders

Unless otherwise authorized in the Credit, banks will only accept a transport document issued by a freight forwarder if it appears on its face to indicate:

i) the name of the freight forwarder as a carrier or multimodal transport operator and to have been signed or otherwise authenticated by the freight forwarder as carrier or multimodal transport operator, or

ii) the name of the carrier or multimodal transport operator and to have been signed or otherwise authenticated by the freight forwarder as a named agent for or on behalf of the carrier or multimodal transport operator.

Article 31. "On Deck", "Shipper's Load and Count", Name of Consignor

Unless otherwise stipulated in the Credit, banks will accept a transport document which:

i) does not indicate, in the case of carriage by sea or by more than one means of conveyance including carriage by sea, that the goods are or will be loaded on deck. Nevertheless, banks will accept a transport document which contains a provision that the goods may be carried on deck, provided that it does not specifically state that they are or will be loaded on deck, and/or

ii) bears a clause on the face thereof such as "shipper's load and count" or "said by shipper to contain" or words of similar effect, and/or

iii) indicates as the consignor of the goods a party other than the beneficiary of the Credit.

Article 32. Clean Transport Documents

a. A clean transport document is one which bears no clause or notation which expressly declares a defective condition of the goods and/or the packaging.

b. Banks will not accept transport documents bearing such clauses or notations unless the Credit expressly stipulates the clauses or notations which may be accepted.

c. Banks will regard a requirement in a Credit for a transport document to bear the clause "clean on board" as complied with if such transport document meets the requirements of this Article and of Articles 23, 24, 25, 26, 27, 28 or 30.

Article 33. Freight Payable/Prepaid Transport Documents

a. Unless otherwise stipulated in the Credit, or inconsistent with any of the documents presented under the Credit, banks will accept transport documents stating that freight or transportation charges (hereafter referred to as "freight") have still to be paid.

b. If a Credit stipulates that the transport document has to indicate that freight has been paid or prepaid, banks will accept a transport document on which words clearly indicating payment or prepayment of freight appear by stamp or otherwise, or on which payment or prepayment of freight is indicated by other means. If the Credit requires courier charges to be paid or prepaid banks will also accept a transport document issued by a courier or expedited delivery service evidencing that courier charges are for the account of a party other than the consignee.

c. The words "freight pre-payable" or "freight to be prepaid" or words of similar effect, if appearing on transport documents, will not be accepted as constituting evidence of the payment of freight.

d. Banks will accept transport documents bearing reference by stamp or otherwise to costs additional to the freight, such as costs of, or disbursements incurred in connection with, loading, unloading or similar operations, unless the conditions of the credit specifically prohibit such reference.

Article 34. Insurance Documents

a. Insurance documents must appear on their face to be issued and signed by insurance companies or underwriters or their agents.

b. If the insurance document indicates that it has been issued in more than one original, all the originals must be presented unless otherwise authorized in the Credit.

c. Cover notes issued by brokers will not be accepted, unless specifically authorized in the Credit.

d. Unless otherwise stipulated in the Credit, banks will accept an insurance certificate or a declaration under an open cover pre-signed by insurance companies or underwriters or their agents. If a Credit specifically calls for an insurance certificate or a declaration under an open cover, banks will accept, in lieu thereof, an insurance policy.

e. Unless otherwise stipulated in the Credit, or unless it appears from the insurance document that the cover is effective at the latest from the date of loading on board or dispatch or taking in charge of the goods, banks will not accept an insurance document which bears a date of issuance later than the date of loading on board or dispatch or taking in charge as indicated in such transport document.

f. i) Unless otherwise stipulated in the Credit, the insurance document must be expressed in the same currency as the Credit.

ii) Unless otherwise stipulated in the Credit, the minimum amount for which the insurance document must indicate the insurance cover to have been effected is the CIF (cost, insurance and freight ("named port of destination")) or CIP (carriage and insurance paid to ("named place of destination")) value of the goods, as the case may be, plus 10%, but only when the CIF or CIP value can be determined from the documents on their face. Otherwise, banks will accept as such minimum amount 110% of the amount for which payment, acceptance or negotiation is requested under the Credit, or 110% of the gross amount of the invoice, whichever is the greater.

Article 35. Type of Insurance Cover

a. Credits should stipulate the type of insurance required and, if any, the additional risks which are to be covered. Imprecise terms such as "usual risks" or "customary risks" shall not be used, if they are used, banks will accept insurance documents as presented, without responsibility for any risks not being covered.

b. Failing specific stipulations in the Credit, banks will accept insurance documents as presented, without responsibility for any risks not being covered.

c. Unless otherwise stipulated in the Credit, banks will accept an insurance document which indicates that the cover is subject to a franchise or on excess (deductible).

Article 36. All Risks Insurance Cover

There a Credit stipulates "insurance against all risks", banks will accept an insurance document which contains any "all risks" notation or clause, whether or not bearing the heading "all risks", even if the insurance document indicates that certain risks are excluded, without responsibility for any risk (s) not being covered.

Article 37. Commercial Invoices

a. Unless otherwise stipulated in the Credit, commercial invoices;

i) must appear on their face to be issued by the Beneficiary named in the Credit (except as provided in Article 48), and

ii) must be made out in the name of the Applicant (except as provided in sub-Article 48 (h), and

iii) need not be signed.

b. Unless otherwise stipulated in the Credit, banks may refuse commercial invoices issued for amounts in excess of the amount permitted by the Credit. Nevertheless, if a bank authorized to pay, incur a deferred payment undertaking, accept Draft (s), or negotiate under a Credit accepts such invoices, its decision will be binding upon all parties, provided that such bank has not paid, incurred a deferred payment undertaking, accepted Draft (s) or negotiated for an amount in excess of that permitted by the Credit.

c. The description of the goods in the commercial invoice must correspond with the description in the Credit. In all other documents, the goods may be described in general terms not inconsistent with the description of the goods in the Credit.

Article 38. Other Documents

If a Credit calls for an attestation or certification of weight in the case of transport other than by sea, bank will accept a weight stamp or declaration of weight which appears to have been superimposed on the transport document by the carrier or his agent unless the Credit specifically stipulates that the attestation or certification of weight must be by means of a separate document.

E. MISCELLANEOUS PROVISIONS

Article 39. Allowances in Credit Amount, Quantity and Unit Price

a. The words "about", "approximately", "circa" or similar expressions used in connection with the amount of the Credit or the quantity or the unit price stated in the Credit are to be construed as allowing a difference not to exceed 10% more or 10% less than the amount or the quantity or the unit price to which they refer.

b. Unless a Credit stipulates that the quantity of the goods specified must not be exceeded or reduced, a tolerance of 5% more or 5% less will be permissible, always provided that the amount of the drawings does not exceed the amount of the Credit. This tolerance does not apply when the Credit stipulates the quantity in terms of a stated number of packing units or individual items.

c. Unless a Credit which prohibits partial shipments stipulates otherwise, or unless sub-Article (b) above is applicable, a tolerance of 5%

less in the amount of the drawing will be permissible, provided that if the Credit stipulates the quantity of the goods, such quantity of goods is shipped in full, and if the Credit stipulates a unit price, such price is not reduced. This provision does not apply when expressions referred to in sub-Article (a) above are used in the Credit.

Article 40. Partial Shipments/Drawings

a. Partial drawings and/or shipments are allowed, unless the Credit stipulates otherwise.

b. Transport documents which appear on their face to indicate that shipment has been made on the same means of conveyance and for the same journey, provided they indicate the same destination, will not be regarded as covering partial shipments, even if the transport documents indicate different dates of shipment and/or different ports of loading, places of taking in charge, or dispatch.

c. Shipments made by post or by courier will not be regarded as partial shipments if the post receipts or certificates of posting or courier's receipts or dispatch notes appear to have been stamped, signed or otherwise authenticated in the place from which the Credit stipulates the goods are to be dispatched, and on the same date.

Article 41. Instalment Shipments/Drawings

If drawings and/or shipments by instalments within given periods are stipulated in the Credit and any instalment is not drawn and/or shipped within the period allowed for that instalment, the Credit ceases to be available for that and any subsequent instalments, unless otherwise stipulated in the Credit.

Article 42. Expiry Date and Place for Presentation of Documents

a. All Credits must stipulate an expiry date and a place for presentation of documents for payment, acceptance, or with the exception of freely negotiable Credits, a place for presentation of documents for negotiation. An expiry date stipulated for payment, acceptance or negotiation will be construed to express an expiry date for presentation of documents.

b. Except as provided in sub-Article 44 (a), documents must be presented on or before such expiry date.

c. If an Issuing Bank states that the Credit is to be available "for one month", "for six months", or the like, but does not specify the date from which the time is to run, the date of issuance of the Credit by the Issuing Bank will be deemed to be the first day from which such time is to run. Banks should discourage indication of the expiry date of the Credit in this manner.

Article 43. Limitation on the Expiry Date

a. In addition to stipulating an expiry date for presentation of documents, every Credit which calls for a transport document (s) should also stipulate a specified period of time after the date of shipment during which presentation must be made in compliance with the terms and conditions of the Credit. If no such period of time is stipulated, banks will not accept documents presented to them later than 21 days after the date of shipment. In any event, documents must be presented not later than the expiry date of the Credit.

b. In cases in which sub-Article 40 (b) applies, the date of shipment will be considered to be the latest shipment date on any of the transport documents presented.

Article 44. Extension of Expiry Date

a. If the expiry date of the Credit and/or the last day of the period of time for presentation of documents stipulated by the Credit or applicable by virtue of Article 43 falls on a day on which the bank to which presentation has to be made is closed for reasons other than those referred to in Article 17, the stipulated expiry date and/or the last day of the period of time after the date of shipment for presentation of documents, as the case may be, shall be extended to the first following day on which such bank is open.

b. The latest date for shipment shall not be extended by reason of the extension of the expiry date and/or the period of time after the date of shipment for presentation of documents in accordance with sub-Article (a) above. If no such latest date for shipment is stipulated in the Credit or amendments thereto, banks will not accept transport documents indicating a date of shipment later than the expiry date stipulated in the Credit or amendments thereto.

c. The bank to which presentation is made on such first following business day must provide a statement that the documents were presented within the time limits extended in accordance with sub – Article 44 (a) of the Uniform Customs and Practice for Documentary Credits, 1993 Revision, ICC Publication No. 500.

Article 45. Hours of Presentation

Banks are under no obligation to accept presentation of documents outside their banking hours.

Article 46. General Expressions as to Dates for Shipment

a. Unless otherwise stipulated in the Credit, the expression "shipment" used in stipulating an earliest and/or a latest date for shipment will be understood to include expressions such as, "loading on board", "dis-patch," "accepted for carriage", "date of post receipt", "date of pick-up" and the like, and in the case of a credit calling for a multimodal transport document the expression "taking in charge".

b. Expressions such as "prompt", "immediately", "as soon as possible", and the like should not be used. If they are used, banks will disregard them.

c. If the expression "on or about" or similar expressions are used, banks will interpret them as a stipulation that shipment is to be made during the period from five days before to five days after the specified date, both end days included.

Article 47. Date Terminology for Periods of Shipment

a. The words "to", "until", "till", "from" and words of similar import applying to any date or period in the Credit referring to shipment will be understood to include the date mentioned.

b. The word "after" will be understood to exclude the date mentioned.

c. The terms "first half", "second half" of a month shall be construed respectively as the 1st to the 15th, and the 16th to the last day of such month, all dates inclusive.

d. The terms "beginning", "middle", or "end" of a month shall be construed respectively as the 1st to the 10th, the 11th to the 20th, and the 21st to the last day of such month, all dates inclusive.

F. TRANSFERABLE CREDIT

Article 48. Transferable Credit

a. A transferable Credit is a Credit under which the Beneficiary

(First Beneficiary) may request the bank authorized to pay, incur a deferred payment undertaking, accept or negotiate (the "Transferring Bank"), or in the case of a freely negotiable Credit, the bank specifically authorized in the Credit as a Transferring Bank, to make the Credit available in whole or in part to one or more other Beneficiary (ies) (Second Beneficiary (ies)).

b. A Credit can be transferred only if it is expressly designated as "transferable" by the Issuing Bank. Terms such as "divisible", "fractionable", "assignable", and "transmissible" do not render the Credit transferable. If such terms are used they shall be disregarded.

c. A Transferring Bank shall be under no obligation to effect such transfer except to the extent and in the manner expressly consented to by such bank.

d. At the time of making a request for transfer and prior to transfer of the Credit, the First Beneficiary must irrevocably instruct the Transferring Bank whether or not he retains the right to refuse to allow the Transferring Bank to advise amendments to the Second Beneficiary (ies). If the Transferring Bank consents to the transfer under these conditions, it must, at the time of transfer, advise the Second Beneficiary (ies) of the First Beneficiary's instructions regarding amendments.

e. If a Credit is transferred to more than one Second Beneficiary (ies), refusal of an amendment by one or more Second Beneficiary (ies) does not invalidate the acceptance (s) by the other Second Beneficiary (ies) with respect to whom the Credit will be amended accordingly. With respect to the Second Beneficiary (ies) who rejected the amendment, the Credit will remain unamended.

f. Transferring Bank charges in respect of transfers including commissions, fees, costs or expenses are payable by the First Beneficiary, unless otherwise agreed. If the Transferring Bank agrees to transfer the

Credit it shall be under no obligation to effect the transfer until such charges are paid.

g. Unless otherwise stated in the Credit, a transferable Credit can be transferred once only. Consequently, the Credit cannot be transferred at the request of the Second Beneficiary to any subsequent Third Beneficiary. For the purpose of this Article, a retransfer to the First Beneficiary does not constitute a prohibited transfer. Fractions of a transferable Credit (not exceeding in the aggregate the amount of the Credit) can be transferred separately, provided partial shipments/drawings are not prohibited, and the aggregate of such transfers will be considered as constituting only one transfer of the Credit.

h. The Credit can be transferred only on the terms and conditions specified in the original Credit, with the exception of:

– the amount of the Credit,

– any unit price stated therein,

– the expiry date,

– the last date for presentation of documents in accordance with Article 43,

– the period for shipment,

any or all of which may be reduced or curtailed.

The percentage for which insurance cover must be effected may be increased in such a way as to provide the amount of cover stipulated in the original Credit, or these Articles. In addition, the name of the First Beneficiary can be substituted for that of the Applicant, but if the name of the Applicant is specifically required by the original Credit to appear in any document (s) other than the invoice, such requirement must be fulfilled.

i. The First Beneficiary has the right to substitute his own invoice (s) (and Draft (s)) for those of the Second Beneficiary (ies), for amounts not in excess of the original amount stipulated in the Credit and for the original unit prices if stipulated in the Credit, and upon such substitution of invoice (s) (and Draft (s)) the First Beneficiary can draw under the Credit for the difference, if any, between his voice (s) and the Second Beneficiary's (ies') invoice (s).

When a Credit has been transferred and the First Beneficiary is to supply his own invoice (s) (and Draft (s)) in exchange for the Second Beneficiary's (ies') invoice (s) (and Draft (s)) but fails to do so on first demand, the Transferring Bank has the right to deliver to the Issuing Bank the documents received under the transferred Credit, including the Second Beneficiary's (ies') invoice (s) (and Draft (s)) without further responsibility to the First Beneficiary.

j. The First Beneficiary may request that payment or negotiation be effected to the Second Beneficiary (ies) at the place to which the Credit has been transferred up to and including the expiry date of the Credit, unless the original Credit expressly states that it may not be made available for payment or negotiation at a place other than that stipulated in the Credit. This is without prejudice to the First Beneficiary's right to substitute subsequently his own invoice (s) (and Draft (s)) for those of the Second Beneficiary (ies) and to claim any difference due to him.

G. ASSIGNMENT OF PROCEEDS

Article 49. Assignment of Proceeds

The fact that a Credit is not stated to be transferable shall not affect the Beneficiary's right to assign any proceeds to which he may be, or may become, entitled under such Credit, in accordance with the provisions of the applicable law. This Article relates only to the assignment of proceeds and not to the assignment of the right to perform under the Credit itself.

附录二《跟单信用证统一惯例（1993年修订本）》（国际商会第500号出版物）

A. 总则和定义

第一条　统一惯例的适用范围

跟单信用证统一惯例，1993年修订本，国际商会第500号出版物，适用于所有在正文中表明按本惯例办理的跟单信用证（包括本惯例适用范围内的备用信用证）。除非信用证中另有规定，本惯例对一切有关当事人均具有约束力。

第二条　信用证的意义

就本惯例而言，“跟单信用证”和“备用信用证”（以下统称“信用证”）意指一项约定，不论其如何命名或描述，系指一家银行（“开证行”）以客户（“申请人”）的要求和指示或以其自身的名义，在与信用证条款相符的条件下，凭规定的单据：

Ⅰ. 向第三者（“受益人”）或其指定人付款，或承兑并支付受益人出具的汇票，或

Ⅱ. 授权另一家银行付款，或承兑并支付该汇票，或

Ⅲ. 授权另一家银行议付。

就本惯例而言，一家银行在不同国家设立的分支机构均视为另一家银行。

第三条　信用证与合同

a. 就性质而言，信用证与可能作为其依据的销售合同或其他合同，是相互独立的交易。即使信用证中提及该合同，银行亦与该合同完全无关，且不受其约束。因此，一家银行做出付款、承兑并支付汇票或议付及/或履行信用证项下其他义务的承诺，不受申请人与开证行或与受益人之间在已有关系下产生索偿或抗

辩的制约。

b. 受益人在任何关系下，不得利用银行之间或申请人与开证行之间的契约关系。

第四条　单据与货物/服务/行为

在信用证业务中，各有关当事人所处理的只是单据，而不是单据所涉及的货物、服务及/或其他行为。

第五条　开立或修改信用证的指示

a. 信用证的开证指示、信用证本身、对信用证的修改指示或修改本身必须完整和明确。

为防止混淆和误解，银行应劝阻下列意图：

Ⅰ. 在信用证或其任何修改中，加注过多细节；

Ⅱ. 在指示开立、通知或保兑一个信用证时，引用先前开立的信用证（参照前证），而该前证受到已被接受及/或未被接受的修改所约束。

b. 有关开立信用证的一切指示和信用证本身，如有修改时，有关修改的一切指示和修改本身都必须明确表明据以付款、承兑或议付的单据。

B. 信用证的形式与通知

第六条　可撤销信用证与不可撤销信用证

a. 信用证可以是：

Ⅰ. 可撤销的，或

Ⅱ. 不可撤销的。

b. 因此信用证应明确注明是可撤销的或是不可撤销的。

c. 如无此项注明，应视为不可撤销的。

第七条　通知行的责任

a. 信用证可经另一家银行（“通知行”）通知受益人，而通知行无须承担责任。如通知行决定通知信用证，它应合理审慎地核审所通知信用证的表面真实性。如通知行决定不通知信用证，它必须毫不延误地告知开证行。

b. 如通知行不能确定信用证的表面真实性，它必须毫不延误地告知从其收到该指示的银行，说明它不能确定该信用证的真实性。如通知行仍决定通知该信用证，必须告知受益人它不能核对信用证的真实性。

第八条　信用证的撤销

a. 可撤销的信用证可以由开证行随时修改或撤销，不必事先通知受益人。

b. 然而，开证行必须：

Ⅰ. 对办理可撤销信用证项下即期付款、承兑或议付的另一家银行，在其收到修改或撤销通知之前已凭表面与信用证条款相符的单据做出的任何付款、承兑或议付，予以偿付。

Ⅱ. 对办理可撤销信用证项下延期付款的另一家银行，在其收到修改或撤销通知之前已接受表面与信用证条款相符的单据，予以偿付。

第九条　开证行与保兑行的责任

a. 对不可撤销的信用证而言，在其规定的单据全部提交指定银行或开证行，并符合信用证条款的条件下，便构成开证行的确定承诺：

Ⅰ. 对即期付款的信用证——即期付款。

Ⅱ. 对延期付款的信用证——按信用证规定所确定的到期日付款。

Ⅲ. 对承兑信用证。

(a) 凡由开证行承兑者——承兑受益人所出具的以开证行为付款人的汇票，并于到期日支付票款，

或

(b) 凡由另一售票银行承兑者——如信用证内规定的受票银行对于以其为付款人的汇票不予承兑，应由开证行承兑并在到期日支付受益人出具的以开证行为付款人的汇票；或者，如受票银

行对汇票已承兑，但到期不付，则开证行应予支付；

Ⅳ. 对议付信用证——根据受益人依照信用证出具的汇票及/或提交的单据向出票人及/或善意持票人履行付款，不得追索。开立信用证时不应以申请人作为汇票付款人。如信用证仍规定汇票付款人为申请人，银行将视此汇票为附加的单据。

b. 根据开证行的授权或要求另一家银行（“保兑行”）对不可撤销信用证加具保兑，当信用证规定的单据提交到保兑行或任何另一家指定银行时，在完全符合信用证规定的情况下则构成保兑行在开证行之外的确定承诺：

Ⅰ. 对即期付款的信用证——即期付款；

Ⅱ. 对延期付款的信用证——按信用证规定所确定的到期日付款；

Ⅲ. 对承兑信用证。

（a）凡由保兑行承兑者——承兑受益人出具的以保兑行为付款人的汇票，并于到期日支付票款，

或

（b）凡由另一售票银行承兑者——如信用证规定的受票银行对于以其为付款人的汇票不予承兑，应由保兑行承兑并在到期日支付受益人出具的以保兑行为付款人的汇票，或者，如受票银行对汇票已承兑但到期不付，则保兑行应予支付。

Ⅳ. 对议付信用证——根据受益人依照信用证出具的汇票及/或提交的单据，向出票人及/或提交的单据，向出票人及/或善意持票人予以支付，不得追索。开立信用证时不应以申请人作为汇票付款人。如信用证仍规定汇票付款人为申请人，银行将视此汇票为附加的单据。

c.

Ⅰ. 如开证行授权或要求另一家银行对信用证加具保兑，而该银行不准备照办时，它必须毫不延误地告知开证行。

Ⅱ. 除非开证行在其授权或要求加具保兑的指示中另有规

定，通知行可以不加保兑并将未经保兑的信用证通知受益人。

d.

Ⅰ. 除第四十八条另有规定外，未经开证行、保兑行（如有）以及受益人同意，不可撤销信用证既不能修改也不能撤销。

Ⅱ. 自发出信用证修改之时起，开证行就不可撤销地受其所发出修改的约束。保兑行可将其保兑扩展至修改，且自其通知该修改之时起，即不可撤销地受修改的约束。然而，保兑行可选择仅将修改通知受益人而不对其加具保兑，但必须毫不延误地将此通知开证行和受益人。

Ⅲ. 在受益人向通知修改的银行表示接受该修改之前，原信用证（或先前已接受修改的信用证）的条款对受益人仍然有效。受益人应提供接受或拒绝接受修改的通知。如受益人未提供上述通知，当它提交给指定银行或开证行的单据与信用证以及尚未表示接受的修改的要求一致时，则该事实即视为受益人已经做出接受修改的通知，并从此时起，该信用证已做修改。

Ⅳ. 对同意修改通知中的修改内容不允许部分接受，因而，部分接受修改内容当属无效。

第十条　信用证的种类

a. 一切信用证均须明确表示它适用于即期付款、延期付款、承兑抑或议付。

b.

Ⅰ. 除非信用证规定只能由开证行办理，一切信用证均须指定某家银行（“指定银行”）并授权其付款、承担延期付款责任、承兑汇票或议付。对自由议付的信用证，任何银行均为指定银行。

单据必须提交给开证行或保兑行（如有）或其他任何指定银行。

Ⅱ. 议付意指被授权议付的银行对汇票及/或单据付出对价。仅审核单据而未付出对价并不构成议付。

c. 除非指定银行是保兑行，指定银行对开证行指定其付款、承担延期付款责任、承兑汇票或议付并不承担责任。除非指定银行已明确同意并告知受益人，否则，它收受及/或审核及/或转交单据的行为，并不意味着它对付款、承担延期付款责任、承兑汇票或议付负有责任。

d. 如开证行指定另一家银行、或允许任何银行议付、或授权或要求另一家银行加具保兑，开证行即分别授权上述银行凭表面与信用证条款相符的单据办理付款、承兑汇票或者议付，并保证依照本惯例对上述银行予以偿付。

第十一条　电讯传递与预先通知的信用证

a.

Ⅰ. 当开证行使用经证实的电讯方式指示通知行通知信用证或信用证修改时，该电讯即视为有效的信用证文件或有效的修改，不应寄送证实书。如仍寄送证实书，则该证实书无效，且通知行没有义务将证实书与所收到的以电讯方式传递的有效信用证文件或有效的修改进行核对。

Ⅱ. 若该电讯声明“详情后告”（或类似词语）或声明寄送证实书将是有效的信用证文件或有效的修改，则该电讯将是有效的信用证文件或修改。开证行必须毫不延误地向通知行寄送有效的信用证文件或有效的修改。

b. 如一家银行利用一家通知行的服务将信用证通知给受益人，它也必须利用同一家银行的服务通知修改。

c. 唯有准备开立有效信用证或修改的开证行，才可以对不可撤销信用证或修改发出预先通知书。除非开证行在其预先通知书中另有规定，发出预先通知的开证行应不可撤销地保证毫不延误地开出或修改信用证，且条款不能与预先通知书相矛盾。

第十二条　不完整或不清楚的指示

如所收到的有关通知、保兑或修改信用证的指示不完整或不清楚，被要求执行该指示的银行可以给受益人一份仅供参考，且不负任何责任的初步通知。该预先通知书应清楚地声明本通知书仅供参考，且通知行不承担责任。但通知行必须将所采取的行动告知开证行，并要求开证行提供必要的内容。

开证行必须毫不延误地提供必要的内容。唯有通知行收到完整明确的指示，并准备执行时，信用证方得通知、保兑或修改。

C. 责任与义务

第十三条　审核单据的标准

a. 银行必须合理小心地审核信用证规定的一切单据，以确定是否表面与信用证条款相符合。本惯例所体现的国际标准银行实务是确定信用证所规定的单据表面与信用证条款相符合的依据。单据之间表面互不一致，即视为表面与信用证条款不符。

银行将不审核信用证没有规定的单据。如果银行收到此类单据，应退还交单人或将其照转，并对此不承担责任。

b. 开证行、保兑行（如有），或代其行事的指定银行，应有各自的合理时间——不得超过从其收到单据的翌日起算7个银行工作日——来审核单据，以决定接受或拒绝接受单据，并相应地通知寄送单据的一方。

c. 如信用证含有某些条件而未列明须提交与之相符的单据，银行将认为未列明此条件，且对此不予理会。

第十四条　不符点单据与通知

a. 当开证行授权另一家银行依据表面符合信用证条款的单据付款、承担延期付款责任、承兑汇票或议付时，开证行和保兑行（如有），承担下列责任：

Ⅰ. 对已付款、已承担延期付款责任、已承兑汇票或已议付指定银行予以偿付。

Ⅱ. 接受单据。

b. 开证行及/或保兑行（如有），或代其行事的指定银行，当收到单据时，必须仅以单据为依据，确定单据是否表面与信用用证条款相符。如单据表面与信用证条款不符，可以拒绝接受。

c. 如开证行确定单据表面与信用证条款不符，它可以自行确定联系申请人对不符点予以接受，但是，不能借此延长第十三条（b）款规定的期限。

d.

Ⅰ. 如开证行及/或保兑行（如有），或代其行事的指定银行，决定拒绝接受单据，它必须毫不延误地以电讯方式，如不可能，则以其他快捷方式通知此事，但不得迟于收到单据的翌日起算第7个银行工作日。该通知应发给寄送单据的银行，或者，如直接从受益人处收到单据，则通知受益人。

Ⅱ. 该通知必须说明银行凭以拒绝接受单据的全部不符点，并说明单据已代为保管听候处理，或已退交单人。

Ⅲ. 然后，开证行及/或保兑行（如有），便有权向交单行索回已经给予该银行的任何偿付款项及利息。

e. 如开证行及/或保兑行（如有），未能按照本条文的规定办理及/或未能代为保管单据听候处理，或经退交单人，开证行及/或保兑行（如有）将无权宣称单据与信用证条款不符。

f. 如寄单行向开证行及/或保兑行（如有）指出单据中的不符点，或通知行为此已经凭赔偿担保付款、承担延期付款责任、承兑汇票或议付，开证行及/或保兑行（如有），并不因此而解除其在本条文项下的任何义务。此项保留或赔偿担保仅涉及寄单行与为之保留，或者，提供或代为提供赔偿担保一方之间的关系。

第十五条 对单据有效性的免责

银行对于任何单据的形式、完整性、准确性、真伪性或法律效力，或对于单据上规定的或附加的一般性及/或特殊性条件，概不负责；银行对于任何单据中有关的货物描述、数量、重量、质量、状况、包装、交货、价值或存在，对于货物的发运人、承运人、运输行、收货人或保险承保人或其他任何人的诚信、行为及/或疏忽、清偿能力、执行能力或信誉也概不负责。

第十六条　对文电传递的免责

银行对于任何文电、信函或单据传递中发生的延误及/或遗失所造成的后果，或对于任何电讯传递过程中发生的延误、残缺或其他差错，概不负责。银行对于专门性术语的翻译及/或解释上的差错，也不负责。银行保留将信用证条款原文照转而不翻译的权利。

第十七条　不可抗力

银行对于天灾、暴动、骚乱、叛乱、战争或银行本身无法控制的任何其他原因，或对于任何罢工或停工而中断营业所引起的一切后果，概不负责。除非经特别授权，银行在恢复营业后，对于在营业中断期间已逾期的信用证，将不再据以进行付款、承担延期付款责任、承兑汇票或议付。

第十八条　对被指示方行为的免责

a. 为执行申请人的指示，银行利用另一家银行或其他银行的服务，是代申请人办理的，其一切风险由申请人承担。

b. 即使银行主动选择其他银行办理业务，如发出的指示未被执行，银行对此亦不负责。

c.

Ⅰ. 一方指示另一方提供服务时，被指示一方因执行指示而产生的一切费用由指示方承担，包括手续费、费用、成本费或其他开支。

Ⅱ. 当信用证规定上述费用由指示方以外的一方负担，而费用未能收回时，亦不能免除最终仍由指示方支付此类费用的责任。

d. 申请人应受外国法律和惯例加诸银行的一切义务和责任的约束，并承担赔偿之责。

第十九条　银行间的偿付约定

a. 开证行如欲通过另一方（“偿付行”）对付款行、承兑行或议付行（均称“索偿行”）履行偿付时，开证行应及时给偿付行对此类索偿予以偿付的适当指示或授权。

b. 开证行不应要求索偿行向偿付行提供与信用证条款相符的证明。

c. 如索偿行未能从偿付行得到偿付，开证行不能解除自身偿付责任。

d. 如偿付行未能在首次索偿时进行偿付，或未能按信用证规定或另行约定的方式进行偿付，开证行应对索偿行的利息损失负责。

e. 偿付行的费用应由开证行承担。然而，如费用由其他方承担，开证行有责任在原信用证中和偿付授权书中予以注明。如偿付行的费用系由其他方承担，该费用应在支付信用证项下款项时向索偿行收取。

D. 单据

第二十条　对出单人而言的模糊用语

a. 不应使用诸如“第一流”、“著名”、“合格”、“独立”、“正式”、“有资格”、“当地”及类似意义的词语来描述信用证项下应提交的任何单据的出单人。如信用证中含有此类词语，只要所提交的单据表面与信用证其他条款相符，且并非由受益人出具，银行将照予接受。

b. 除非信用证中另有规定，只要单据注明为正本，如必要时，已加签字，银行业将接受下列方法制作或看来是按该方法制作的单据作为正本单据：

Ⅰ. 影印、自动或电脑处理；

Ⅱ. 复写；

单据签字可以手签，也可以签样印制、穿孔签字、盖章、符号表示或其他任何机械或电子证实的方法处理。

c.

Ⅰ. 除非信用证另有规定，银行将接受表明副本字样或没有标明正本字样的单据作为副本单据，副本单据无需签字。

Ⅱ. 如信用证要求多份单据，诸如“一式两份”、“两张”、“两份”等，可以提交一份正本，其余分数以副本来满足。但单据本身另有显示者除外。

d. 除非信用证另有规定，当信用证含有要求证实单据、使单据生效、使单据合法、签证单据、证明单据或对单据有类似要求的条件时，该条件可由在单据上签字、标注、盖章或标签来满足，只要单据表面已满足上述条件即可。

第二十一条　对出单人或单据内容未作规定

当要求提供运输单据、保险单据和商业发票以外的单据时，信用证中应规定该单据的出单人及其措辞或内容。如信用证对此未作规定，只要所提交单据的内容与提交的其他规定单据不矛盾，银行将接受此类单据。

第二十二条　出单日期与信用证日期

除非信用证种类有规定，银行将接受出单日期早于信用证日期的单据，但该单据必须在信用证和本惯例规定的期限内提交。

第二十三条　海洋运输提单

a. 如信用证要求港至港运输单据，除非信用证另有规定，银行将接受下述单据，不论其称谓如何：

Ⅰ. 表面注明承运人的名称，并由下列人员签字或以其他方式证实：

——承运人或作为承运人的具名代理或代表，或

——船长或作为船长的具名代理或代表。

承运人或船长的任何签字或证实，必须表明“承运人”或“船长”的身份。代理人代表承运人或船长签字或证实时也必须标明所代表的委托人的名称和身份。即注明代理人是代表承运人或船长签字或证实的，

及

Ⅱ. 注明货物已装船或已装具名船只。

已装船或已装具名船中，只由提单上印就的“货物已装上具名船只”或“货物已装运具名船只”的词语来表示，在此情况下，提单的出具日期即视为装船日期与装运日期。

在所有其他情况下装上具名船只，必须以提单上注明货物装船日期的批注来证实。在此情况下，装船批注日期即视为装运日期。

当提单含有“预期船”字样或类似有关限定船只的词语时，装上具名船只必须由提单上的装船批注来证实。在此情况下，装船批注日期即视为装运日期。

如提单注明的收货地或接受监管地与装货港不同，已装船批注仍须注明信用证规定的装货港和实际装货船名，即使已装货船只的名称与提单注明的船只名称一致，亦是如此。本规定还适用于任何由提单上印就的装船词语来表示装船情况，

及

Ⅲ. 注明信用证规定的装货港和卸货港，尽管提单上可能有下述情况：

(a) 注明不同于装货港的接受监管地及/或不同于卸货港的最终目的地，

及/或

(b) 含有“预期”或类似有关限定装货港，及/或卸货港的标注者，只要单据上表示了信用证规定的装货港及/或卸货港，

及

Ⅳ. 开立全套正本提单可以是仅有一份正本提单或者是一份以上正本提单，

及

Ⅴ. 含有全部承运条件或部分承运条件须参阅提单以外的某一出处或文件（简式/背面空白提单）者，银行对此类承运条件的内容不予审核，

及

Ⅵ. 未注明受租船合约约束及/或未注明承运船只仅以风帆为动力者，

及

Ⅶ. 在所有其他方面均符合信用证规定者。

b. 就本条文而言，转运意指在信用证规定的装货港到卸货港之间的海运过程中，将货物由一艘船卸下再装上另一艘船的运输。

c. 除非信用证禁止转运，只要同一提单包括了海运全程运输，银行将接受注明货物将转运的提单。

d. 即使信用证禁止转运，银行对下列单据予以接受。

Ⅰ. 对注明将发生转运者，只要提单证实有关货物已由集装箱、拖车及/或子母船运输，并且同一提单包括海运全程运输，

及/或

Ⅱ. 含有承运人声明保留转运权力条款者。

第二十四条　非转让的海运单

a. 如信用证要求港至港非转让海运单，除非信用证另有规定，银行将接受下述单据，不论其称谓如何：

Ⅰ. 表面注明承运人名称，并由下列人员签字或以其他方式证实：

——承运人或作为承运人的具名代理或代表，或

——船长或作为船长的具名代理或代表。

承运人或船长的任何签字或证实，必须表明“承运人”或“船长”的身份。代理人代表承运人或船长签字或证实时，也必须表明所代表的委托人的名称和身份，即注明代理人是代表承运人或船长签字或证实的，

及

Ⅱ. 注明货物已装船或已装具名船只。

已装船或已装具名船只，可由非转让海运提单上印证的“货物已装上具名船只”或“货物已装具名船只”的词语来表示，在

此情况下，非转让海运提单的出具日期即视为装船日期或装运日期。

在所有其他情况下，装上具名船只，必须以非转让海运提单上注明货物装船日期的批注来证实。在此情况下，装船批注日期即视为装运日期。

如非转让海运提单含有“预期船”或类似有关限定船只的词语时，装上具名船只必须由非转让海运单上装船批注来证实，该项装船批注除注明货物已装船日期外，还应包括装货的船名，即使实际装货船只的名称为“预期船”亦是如此。

如果非转让海运单注明的收货地或接受监管地与装货港不同，已装船批注中仍须注明信用证规定的装货港和实际装货船名，即使装货船只的名称与非转让海运单上注明的船只一致，亦是如此。本规定适用于任何由非转让海运单上印就的装船词语来表示装船情况，

及

Ⅲ.注明信用证规定的装货港和卸货港，尽管非转让海运单可能有下述情况：

(a) 注明不同于装运港的接受监管地及/或不同于卸货港的最终目的地，

及/或

(b) 含有“预期”或类似有关限定装运港及/或卸货港的标注者，只要单据上表示了信用证规定的装运港及/或卸货港，

及

Ⅳ.开立全套正本提单可以是仅有一份正本提单或者是一份以上正本提单，及

Ⅴ.含有全部承运条件或部分承运条件须参阅非转让海运单以外的某一出处或文件（简式/背面空白的非转让海运单）者，银行对此类承运条件的内容不予审核，

及

Ⅵ. 未注明受租船合约约束及/或未注明承运船只仅以风帆为动力者，

及

Ⅶ. 在所有其他方面均符合信用证规定者。

b. 就本条款而言，转运意指在信用证规定的装货港到卸货港之间的海运全过程中，将货物由一艘船卸下再装上另一艘船的运输。

c. 除非信用证禁止转运，只要同一非转让海运单包括了海运全程运输，银行将接受注明货物将转运的非转让海运单。

d. 即使信用证禁止转运，银行将接受下列非转让海运单：

Ⅰ. 对注明将发生转运者，就只要非转让海运单证实有关货物已由集装箱、拖车及/或子母驳船运输，并且同一非转让海运单包括海运全程运输，

及/或

Ⅱ. 含有承运人声明保留转运权力的条款者。

第二十五条　租船合约提单

a. 如果信用证要求或允许提交租船合约提单，除非信用证另有规定，银行将接受下述单据，不论其称谓如何：

Ⅰ. 含有受租船合约约束的任何批注，

及

Ⅱ. 已由下列人员签字或以其他方式证实：

——船长或作为船长的具名代理或代表，或

——船东或作为船东的具名代理或代表。

船长或船东的任何签字或证实，必须表明“船长”或“船东”的身份。代理人代表船长或船东签字或证实时，亦须表明所代表的委托人的名称和身份，即注明代理人是代表船长或船东签字或证实的，

及

Ⅲ. 注明或不注明承运人的名称，

及

Ⅳ. 注明货物已装船或已装具名船只。

已装船或已装具名船只，可由提单上印就“货物已装上具名船只”或“货物已装运具名船只”的词语来表示，在此情况下，提单的出单日期将视为装运日期。

在所有其他情况下，装上具名船只，必须以提单上注明的货物装船日期的批注来证实，在此情况下，装船批注日期即视为装运日期，

及

Ⅴ. 注明信用证规定的装货港和卸货港，

及

Ⅵ. 开立全套正本提单可以是仅有一份正本提单或者是一份以上正本提单，

及

Ⅶ. 未注明承运船只仅以风帆为动力者，

及

Ⅷ. 在所有其他方面均符合信用证规定者。

b. 即使信用证要求提交与租船合约提单有关的租船合同，银行对该租船合约不予审核，但将予以照转而不承担责任。

第二十六条　多式运输单据

a. 如信用证要求提供至少包括两种不同运输方式（多式运输）的运输单据，除非信用证另有规定，银行将接受下述运输单据，不论其称谓如何：

Ⅰ. 表面注明承运人的名称或多式运输营运人的名称，并由下列人员签字或以其他方式证实：

——承运人或多式运输营运人或作为承运人或多式运输营运人的具名代理或代表，或

——船长或作为船长的具名代理或代表。

承运人或多式运输营运人或船长的任何签名或证实，必须分

别表明“承运人”或“多式运输营运人”或“船长”的身份。代理人代表承运人或多式运输营运人或船长签字或证实时，也必须注明所代表的委托人的名称和身份，即注明代理人是代表承运人或多式运输营运人或船长签字或证实的，

及

Ⅱ. 注明货物已发运、接受监管或已装载者。

发运、接受监管或装载，可在多式运输单据上以文字表明，其出单日期即视为发运、接受监管或装载日期及装运日期。然而，如果单据以盖章或其他方式标明发运、接受监管或装载日期，则此类日期即视为装运日期，

及

Ⅲ.

(a) 注明信用证规定的货物接受监管地，该接受监管地可以不同于装运港、装货机场和装货地，及/或注明信用证规定的最终目的地，该最终目的地可以与卸货港、卸货机场或卸货地不同，

及/或

(b) 含有“预期”或类似限定有关船只及/或装货港及/或卸货港的批注，

及

Ⅳ. 开立全套正本提单可以是仅有一份正本提单或者是一份以上正本提单，

及

Ⅴ. 含有全部承运条件或部分承运条件须参阅多式运输单据以外的某一出处或文件（简式/背面空白的多式运输单据）者，银行对此类承运条件的内容不予审核，

及

Ⅵ. 未注明受租船合约约束及/或未注明承运船只仅以风帆为动力者，

及

Ⅶ. 在所有其他方面均符合信用证规定者。

b. 即使信用证禁止转运，银行也将接受注明转运将发生或可能发生的多式运输单据，只要同一多式运输单据包括运输全程。

第二十七条　空运单据

a. 如果信用证要求空运单据，除非信用证另有规定，银行将接受下列单据，不论其称谓如何：

Ⅰ. 表面注明承运人名称并由下列人员签字或以其他方式证实：

——承运人；或

——作为承运人的具名代理或代表。

承运人的任何签字或证实必须表明承运人的身份。代理人代表承运人签字或证实亦须表明所代表的委托人的名称和身份，即表明代理人是代表承运人签字或证实者，

及

Ⅱ. 注明货物已收妥待运，

及

Ⅲ. 如信用证要求实际发运日期，应对此日期做出专项批注。在空运单据上如此表示的发运日期，即视为装运日期。

就本条款而言，在空运单据的方格（标明“仅供承运人使用”或类似说明）内所表示的有关航班号和起飞日期的信息不能视为发运日期的专项批注。

在所有其他情况下，签发空运单据的日期即视为装运日期，

及

Ⅳ. 注明信用证规定的发运机场及目的地机场，

及

Ⅴ. 开给委托人/发货人的正本空运单据，即使信用证规定全套正本，或有类似意义的词语，

及

Ⅵ. 含有全部承运条件，或其中某些承运条件须参阅空运单以外的某一出处或文件者，银行对此类承运条件的内容将不予审核，

及

Ⅶ. 所在其他方面均符合信用证规定。

b. 就本条款而言，转运意指在信用证规定的起飞机场到目的地机场的运输过程中，将货物从一架飞机上卸下再装到另一架飞机上的运输。

c. 即使信用证禁止转运，银行将接受注明将发生或可能发生转运的空运单据，只要是同一空运单据包括运输全程。

第二十八条　公路、铁路或内河运输单据

a. 如果信用证要求公路、铁路或内河运输单据，除非信用证另有规定，银行将接受所要求的类型的运输单据，不论其称谓如何：

Ⅰ. 表面注明承运人的名称并且已由承运人或作为承运人的具名代理或代表签字或以其他方式证实，及/或载有承运人或作为承运人的具名代理或代表的收妥印章或其他收妥的标志。

承运人的任何签名、证实、收妥印章或其他收妥印章标志，表面须表明承运人的身份，代表承运人签字或证实，亦须表明其所代表的委托人的名称和身份，即注明代理人是代表承运人签字或证实的，

及

Ⅱ. 注明货物已收妥待运、发运或承运或类似意义的词语，除非运输单据盖有收妥印章，运输单据的出具日期即视为装运日期。在加盖收妥印章的情况下，盖章的日期即视为装运日期，

及

Ⅲ. 注明信用证规定的装运地和目的地，

及

Ⅳ. 所有其他方面均符合信用证规定。

b. 如运输单据未注明出具单据份数，银行将接受所提交的运输单据，并视为全套正本，不论运输单据是否注明为正本，银行将作为正本予以接受。

c. 就本条款而言，转运意指在信用证规定的装运地到目的地之间的运输过程中，以不同的运输方式，从一种运输工具卸下再装至另一种运输工具的运输。

d. 即使信用证禁止转运，银行也将接受注明将转运或可能发生转运的公路、铁路或内河运输单据，只要运输的全过程包括在同一运输单据内，并使用同一运输方式。

第二十九条　专递及邮政收据

a. 如果信用证要求邮政收据或投递证明，除非信用证另有规定，银行将接受下述邮政收据或投邮证明：

I. 表面上有信用证规定的装运地或发运地戳记或以其他方式证实并加注日期者，该日期即视为装运或发运日期，

及

II. 所有其他各方面均符合信用证规定。

b. 如信用证要求由专递或快递机构出具证明收到待运货物的单据，除非信用证另有规定，银行将接受下列单据，不论其称谓如何：

I. 表面注明专递/快递机构的名称，并由该具名的专递/快递机构盖戳、签字或以其他方式证实的单据（除非信用证特别规定由指定的专递/快递机构出具单据，银行将接受由任何专递/快递机构出具的单据）。

及

II. 注明取件或收件日期或同义词语者，此日期即视为装运或发运日期。

III. 所有其他各方面均符合信用证规定。

第三十条　运输行出具的运输单据

除非信用证另有授权，银行仅接受运输行出具的具有下列注

明的运输单据：

I. 注明作为承运人或多式运输营运人的运输行的名称，并由作为承运人或多式运输营运人的运输行签字或以其他方式证实，

或

II. 注明承运人或多式运输营运人的名称并由作为承运人或多式运输营运人的具明代理或代表的运输行签字或以其他方式证实。

第三十一条　“货装舱面”，“发货人装载并计数”，发货人名称

除非信用证另有规定，银行将接受下列运输单据：

I. 海运或包括海运在内的一种以上运输方式，未注明货物已装或将装于舱面。然而，运输单据内有货物可能装于舱面的规定，但未特别注明货物已装舱面或将装舱面，银行对该运输单据予以接受，

及/或

II. 含有“发货人装载并计数”或“内容根据发货人报称”或类似文字的条款的运输单据，

及/或

III. 表明以信用证受益人以外的一方为发货人的运输单据。

第三十二条　洁净运输单据

a. 洁净运输单据系指未载有明确宣称货物及/或包装状况有缺陷的条款或批注的运输单据。

b. 除非信用证明确规定可以接受上述条款或批注，银行将不接受载有此类条款或批注的运输单据。

c. 运输单据如符合本条款和第二十三、二十四、二十五、二十六、二十七、二十八或三十条的规定，银行即视为符合信用证中规定在运输单据上载明“洁净已装船”的要求。

第三十三条　运费到付/运费预付的运输单据

a. 除非信用证另有规定，或与信用证项下所提交的任何单据相抵触，银行将接受表明运费或运输费用（以下统称“运费”）待付的运输单据。

b. 如果信用证规定运输单据中必须表明运费付讫或已预付，银行将接受以戳记或以其他方式清楚地表明运费付讫或已预付的词语，或用其他方法表明运费付讫的运输单据。如信用证要求专递费用付讫或预付时，银行也将接受专递或快递机构出具的注明专递费用由收货人以外的一方承担的运输单据。

c. 运输单据上如出现“运费可预付”或“运费应预付”或类似意义的词语，不能视为运费付讫的证明，将不予接受。

d. 银行将接受以戳记或其他方式提及运费以外的附加费用，诸如有关装卸或其他类似作业所引起的费用或开支的运输单据，除非信用证条款明确禁止接受此类运输单据。

第三十四条　保险单据

a. 保险单据从其表面上看，必须是由保险公司或承保人或他们的代理人开立及签署的。

b. 除非信用证另有授权，如保险单据表明所出具正本单据系一份以上，则必须提交全部正本保险单据。

c. 除非信用证特别授权，银行将不接受由保险经纪人签发的暂保单。

d. 除非信用证另有规定，银行将接受由保险公司或承保人或他们的代理人预签的预保单项下保险证明或保险声明。虽然信用证特别要求预保单项下保险证明或保险声明，银行仍可接受保险单以取代前述保险证明或保险声明。

e. 除非信用证另有规定，或除非保险单据表明保险责任最迟于装运或发运或接受监管日起生效，银行对载明签发日期迟于运输单据注明的装船或发运或接受监管日期的保险单据将不予接受。

f.

I. 除非信用证另有规定，保险单据必须使用与信用证相同的货币开立。

II. 除非信用证另有规定，保险单据必须表明的最低投保金额，应为货物的CIF价（成本、保费和运费（……“指定的目的港”））或CIP价（运费和保险费付至（……“指定目的地”））之金额加10%。但这仅限于能从单据表面确定CIF或CIP价值的情况。否则，银行将接受的最低投保金额为信用证要求付款、承兑或议付金额的110%，或发票毛值的110%，两者之中取金额较大者。

第三十五条　投保险别

a. 信用证应规定所需投保险别种类，以及必要的附加险别。诸如“通常险别”或“惯常险别”一类意义不明确的条文不应使用。如使用此类条文，银行当按照所提示的保险单据予以接受，并对未经保险的任何险种不予负责。

b. 如信用证无特别规定，银行当按照所提示的保险单据予以接受，并对未经投保的任何险别不予负责。

c. 除非信用证另有规定，银行将接受表明受免赔率或免赔额约束的保险单据。

第三十六条　投保一切险

当信用证规定“投保一切险”时，银行将接受含有任何“一切险”批注或条文的保险单据，不论其有无“一切险”标题，甚至表明不包括某种险别。银行对未经投保的任何险别不予负责。

第三十七条　商业发票

a. 除非信用证另有规定，商业发票：

I. 必须标明系由信用证中指定的受益人出具（第四十八条所规定者除外），

及

II. 必须做成以申请人的名称为抬头（第四十八条（h）款所

规定者除外），

及

Ⅲ. 无需签字

b. 除非信用证另有规定，银行可拒绝接受金额超过信用证所允许的金额的商业发票。但是，如信用证项下被授权付款、承担延期付款责任、承兑汇票或议付的银行，一旦接受此类发票，只要该银行所做出的付款、承担延期付款责任、已承兑汇票或已议付的金额没有超过信用证所允许的金额，则此项决定对各有关方面均具有约束力。

c. 商业发票中的货物描述，必须与信用证规定相符，其他一切单据则可使用货物统称，但不得与信用证规定的货物描述有抵触。

第三十八条　其他单据

在采用海运以外的运输情况下，如信用证要求重量证明，除非信用证明确规定对此项重量证明必须另行提供单据外，银行将接受承运人或其代理人附加于运输单据上的重量戳记或重量声明。

E. 杂项规定

第三十九条　信用证金额、数量和单价的增减幅度

a. 凡“约”、“大概”、“大约”或类似的词语，用于信用证金额、数量和单价时，应解释为有关金额、数量或单价不超过10%的增减幅度。

b. 除非信用证规定货物的指定数量不得有增减外，在所支付款项不超过信用证金额的条件下，货物数量准许有5%的增减幅度。但是，当信用证规定数量以包装单位或个数计数时，此项增减幅度则不适用。

c. 除非禁止分批装运的信用证另有规定或已适用本条（b）款者，当信用证对货物的数量有规定，且货物已全数装运，以及

当信用证对单价有规定，而此单价又未降低的条件下，允许支取的金额有5%的减幅。如信用证已利用本条（a）款提到的词语，则本规定不适用。

第四十条　分批装运/分批支款

a. 除非信用证另有规定，允许分批支款或分批装运。

b. 运输单据表面注明货物系使用同一运输工具并经同一路线运输的，即使每套运输单据注明的装运日期不同及/或装货港、接受监管地、发运地不同，只要运输单据注明的目的地相同，也不视为分批装运。

c. 货物经邮寄或专递发运，如邮政收据或投邮证明或专递收据或发运通知，是在信用证规定的发货地加盖戳记，或签署或以其他方式证实并且日期相同，则不视为分批装运。

第四十一条　分期装运/分期支款

信用证规定在指定的不同期限内分期支款及/或分期装运，如其中任何一期未按信用证所规定的期限支款及/或装运，则信用证对该期及以后各期均视为无效。信用证另有规定者除外。

第四十二条　到期日及交单地点

a. 所有信用证均须规定一个到期日及一个付款日、承兑交单地点。对议付信用证尚须规定一个议付交单地点，但自由议付信用证除外。规定的付款、承兑或议付的到期日，将视为提交单据的到期日。

b. 除第四十四条（a）款规定外，必须于到期日或到期日之前提交单据。

c. 如开证行注明信用证的有效期限为“一个月”、“六个月”或类似规定，但未指明自何日起算，开证行开立信用证的日期即视为起算日。银行应避免用此种方式注明信用证的到期日。

第四十三条　对到期日的限制

a. 除规定一个交单到期日外，凡要求提交运输单据的信用证，尚须规定一个在装运日后按信用证规定必须交单的特定期限。如未规定该期限，银行将不予接受迟于装运日期后21天提交的单据。但无论如何，提交单据不得迟于信用证的到期日。

b. 如第四十条（b）款适用，所提交的运输单据上的最迟装运日期即视为装运日期。

第四十四条 到期日的顺延

a. 如信用证的到期日及/或信用证规定的交单期限，或第四十三条规定所适用的交单的期限最后一天，适逢接受单据的银行因第十七条规定以外的原因而中止营业，则规定的到期日及/或装运日后一定期限内交单的最后一天，将顺延至该银行开业的第一个营业日。

b. 最迟装运日期不得按照本条（a）款对到期日及/或装运日后交单期限的顺延为由而顺延。如信用证或修改未规定最迟装运日期，银行将不接受表明装运日期迟于信用证或修改规定的到期日的运输单据。

c. 于顺延后的第一个营业日接受单据的银行，必须申明该单据系根据跟单信用证统一惯例，1993年修订本，国际商会第500号出版物的第四十四条（a）款规定的顺延期限内所提交。

第四十五条 交单时间

银行在其营业时间以外，没有接受提交单据的义务。

第四十六条 对装运日期的一般用语

a. 除非信用证另有规定，凡用于规定最早及/或最迟装运日期的“装运”一词的意义，应理解为包括诸如“装船”、“发运”、“接收备运”、“邮政收据日期”、“取件日期”和类似表示，如信用证要求多式运输单据，还包括“接受监管”。

b. 不应使用诸如“迅速”、“立即”、“尽快”之类词语，如使用此类词语，银行将不予置理。

c. 如使用“于或约于”之类词语限定装运日期，银行将视为在所述日期前后各5天内装运，起讫日包括在内。

第四十七条　装运期限的日期用语

a. 诸如“止”、“至”、“直至”、“从”及类似意义的词语用于限定信用证中有关装运的任何日期或期限时，应理解为包括所述的日期。

b. “以后”将理解为不包括所述日期。

c. “上半月”和“下半月”应分别理解为自每月“1日至15日”和“16日至月末最后一天”，包括起讫日。

d. “月初”、“月中”和“月末”应分别理解为每月1日至10日、11日至20日和21日至月末最后一天，包括起讫日期。

F. 可转让信用证

第四十八条　可转让信用证

a. 可转让信用证系指信用证的受益人（第一受益人）可以要求授权付款、承担延期付款责任、承兑或议付的银行（统称“转让银行”），或当信用证是自由议付时，可以要求信用证中特别授权的转让银行，将该信用证全部或部分转让给一个或数个受益人（第二受益人）使用的信用证。

b. 唯有开证行在信用证中明确注明“可转让”，信用证方可转让。使用诸如：“可分割”、“可分开”、“可让渡”和“可转移”之类措辞，并不能使信用证成为可以转让的。如使用此类措辞，可不予以置理。

c. 除非转让银行明确同意其转让范围和转让方式，否则它无义务办理转让。

d. 在申请转让时并且在信用证转出之前，第一受益人必须不可撤销地指示转让银行，说明它是否保留拒绝允许转让银行将修改通知给第二受益人的权利。如转让银行同意按此条件办理转让，它必须在办理转让时，将第一受益人关于修改事项的指示通知第二受益人。

e. 如信用证转让给一个以上的第二受益人，其中一个或几个第二受益人拒绝接受信用证的修改，并不影响其他第二受益人接受修改。对拒绝接受修改的第二受益人而言，该信用证视作未被修改。

f. 除非另有约定，转让银行所涉及转让的费用，包括手续费、费用、成本费或其他开支等，应由第一受益人支付。如果转让银行同意转让信用证，在付清此类费用之前，转让银行没有办理转让的义务。

g. 除非信用证另有说明，可转让信用证只能转让一次。因此，第二受益人不得要求将信用证转让给其后的第三受益人。就本条文而言，在转让给第一受益人，不属被禁止转让的范畴。

只要不禁止分批装运/分批支款，可转让信用证可以分为若干部分予以分别转让（但总和不超过信用证金额），这些转让的总和将被认为该证只转让一次。

h. 信用证只能按原证中规定的条款转让，但下列项目除外：

——信用证金额，

——规定的任何单价，

——到期日，

——根据第四十三条确定的最后交单日期，

——装运期限。

以上任何一项或全部均要减少或缩短。

必须投保的保险金额比例可以增加，以满足原信用证或本惯例规定的保额。

此外，可以用第一受益人的名称替代原信用证申请人的名称。但是，原证中如明确要求原申请人的名称应在除发票以外的单据上出现时，该项要求则必须做到。

i. 第一受益人有权用自己的发票（和汇票）替换第二受益人提交的发票（和汇票），其金额不得超过原信用证金额，如信用证对单价有规定，应按原单价出具发票。经过替换发票（和汇票），第一受益人可以在信用证下支取其发票与第二受益人发票间的可能产生的差额。

当信用证已经转让，并且第一受益人要提供自己的发票（和汇票）以替换第二受益人的发票（和汇票），但第一受益人未能在首次要求时按此办理，则转让银行有权将所收到的已转让信用证项下的单据，包括第二受益人的发票（和汇票）交给开证行，并不再对第一受益人负责。

j. 除非原信用证明确表明不得在原信用证规定以外的地方办理付款或议付，第一受益人可以要求在信用证的受让地，并在信用证到期日以内，对第二受益人履行付款或议付。这样做并不损害第一受益人以自己的发票（和汇票）替换第二受益人的发票（和汇票），并索取两者间应得差额的权利。

G. 款项让渡

第四十九条　款项让渡

信用证未标明可转让，并不影响受益人根据现行法律规定，将信用证项下应得的款项让渡给他人的权利。本条款所涉及的仅是款项的让渡，而不是信用证项下执行权力的让渡。

参 考 文 献

[1] 曲鹏程．2000年国际贸易术语解释通则[M]．北京：中信出版社，2000.

[2] 进出口业务编写组．国际贸易法律惯例规则选编[M]．北京：对外贸易教育出版社，1986.

[3] 陈国武．国际结算与单据制作[M]．上海：上海三联书店，1998.

[4] 陈国武．新编进出口业务300题[M]．北京：中国商务出版社，2004.

[5] 国际商会中国国家委员会．ICC跟单信用证统一惯例（2007修订本）[M]．北京：中国民主法制出版社，2006.

[6] 中国国际商会．跟单信用证统一惯例—国际商会第500号出版物[M]．北京：中国对外经济贸易出版社，1994.